BISHOP AZARIAH

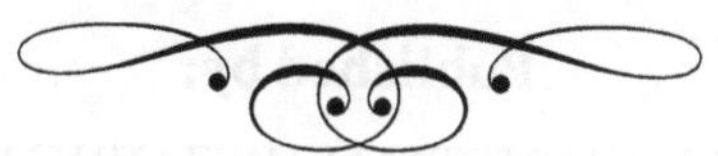

BY

Prof. Rev. D. A. Christadoss
B.A.,L.T.,B.D.,M.Th.

Publisher
TINNEVELLY CHRISTIAN HISTORICAL SOCIETY

BISHOP AZARIAH
in English

Author
Prof. Rev. D. A. Christadoss B. A. , L. T. , B. D. , M. Th.

Published by:

TINNEVELLY CHRISTIAN HISTORICAL SOCIETY
2.2.3(4), North Street,
Bungalow Surandai-627859
Tenkasi district (Tirunelveli)
04633-290401, +91 91767 80001,+91 75388 12218
Email : christianhistorical@gmail.com

Edition:

First -2023

Design & Printing :

TCHS Press

Website :

christianhistoricalsociety.in
tchsportal.co.in

BISHOP AZARIAH

Life & Work Of Right Reverend V. S. Azariah

By

Professor Rev. D. A. Christadoss

B.A., L. T., B. D., M. Th.

Published & Copyright

BY

TINNEVELLY CHRISTIAN HISTORICAL SOCIETY

Donors

Mr.R. Balachandran, Surandai

Dr. B. Davidson Vinodh, Chennai

Tinnevelly Christian Historical Society

Publisher

PUBLISHER'S NOTE

Tinnevelly Christian Historical Society owes much to stalwarts such as Rev. D. A. Christudoss, the author of this book. He is one of the earliest clergy from South India who has systematically recorded the happenings during his lifetime in the vibrant Christian landscape of Tinnevelly and beyond. He has researched, documented, collated and presented narratives with historical accuracy in the form of useful books to the growing Christian community of South India in both Tamil and English. Though he donned many hats, writing remained his passion. It has to be recorded here that one of our team members Sujith stumbled upon the research ledger and handwritten notes of Rev. D. A. Christudoss kept in the Stephen Neil Library in Palayamkottai. The discovery proved to be a great inspiration for all of us to keep on searching and preserving the history of this region and if possible in the high standards set by Rev. Christudoss. We are grateful to God for his pioneering work in recording not only the 'greats' of history but also the 'ordinary' men and women who walked by faith.

This biography of the Apostle of the Dornakal and the first Anglican Bishop, Rev. Vedanayagam Samuel Azariah is a testament to the beautiful penmanship of Rev. Christudass. It was first published in1974 in the Tamil language. We are glad to publish this English translation of the same so that it may reach a wider audience. This book has been an essential resource for many national and international scholars. We offer our sincere thanks to the family of Rev. Christudoss for their consent and support in bringing out this book.

Professor Rev. D. A. Christadoss

Thanks :

Rev. H. John Samuel, Pandaranchettiviali

Rev. A. Jebarathinam, Sambavarvadakarai

Mrs. A. Rhoda Alex,Chennai

Mr. S. Sujith Rex, Alangulam

Mr. G. Manna Selvakumar,Surandai

Professor Rev. D. A. Christadoss

Writer

PREFACE

When I was offered the privilege of writing a brief biography of 'the apostle of Dornakal' Bishop Azariah, I was hesitant because I felt myself unworthy to write about the great man's great life. Bishop Azariah had been credited as 'great among the people of Tirunelveli Diocese'. Among the church leaders described in the annals of the global Church, he is hailed as a unique son of the Indian Church. I got over my initial hesitation thinking that I would be blessed for praising this great man. Then, I set upon the task of writing this book, trusting the grace of God. I thank the many persons who encouraged me by extending their help in many ways, and thus to complete this small book. I extend my heartfelt appreciation and gratitude to Mr. A. J. Azariah, the son of Bishop Azariah, for his excellent co-operation. I thank the committee of the Indian Missionary Society (IMS) for granting me the privilege of authoring this book. I thank the General Secretary and the Treasurer of the IMS for helping me peruse the records, and for funding the book-writing project. When I went to Dornakal, IMS missionaries Rev. R. John G. Samuel and his wife Mrs. P. Koilpillai, and Ms. R. Jayamani enthusiastically helped me gather information that I needed to write this book, and also took me to various churches. I thank them all.

The honorable General Secretary requested me to write this book in a simple language so that ordinary village Christians of this Diocese may be able to read the book and get to know about the great Bishop Azariah, birthed by the Tirunelveli Church. In deference to the lofty wishes of the Hon. General Secretary to make this book readable to the simple village folks, I have written this book in a simple language keeping the village Christians in my mind.

In this book, we have referred to Bishop Azariah and other bishops as Bishops. We have avoided the term 'the Great Shepherd' (*Perayar* in Tamil) used widely today for bishops. Bishop Azariah and other bishops in their time were referred to as '*athiatchar*' (bishops) and not as '*perayar*' (Great Shepherds). To be more precise, among ordinary Christians they were known as '*kankanier*' in Tamil, which means 'overseers'. Only the educated people used the term bishop. The word bishop means 'the important person' or 'the chief person'. The term bishop stems from the word Episcopos, and it means overseer. The term *Athiatchar* used in Tamil for bishop is not a right translation. Moreover, *Athiatchar* is not a Tamil word at all. Nevertheless, we have used the word *Athiatchar* (bishop) in this book because Nellai Christians are familiar with this word.

There is another reason to avoid the term 'the Great Shepherd' for bishop. If we prod our thinking, we can understand that the term 'the Great Shepherd' does not agree with Theology or Church History lessons or the Holy Bible, and it is contrary to these. The word bishop has been translated as overseer in Philippians 1:1; I Tim. 3:2; Titus 1:7; and, I Peter 2:25. The 'Perayar' (or the Great Shepherd or the Chief Shepherd) is Christ only, and not any other. Heb. 13:20; I Peter 5:4; John 10:16. Apart from these, John 10:2-16, Isaiah 40:11, Psalm 23:1-3 and Psalm 80:1 depict Christ as 'the Good Shepherd', 'Shepherd of our souls', and 'the Shepherd of Israel'. Because of the truth that comes out of these verses, may we avoid the term 'the Great Shepherd'.

Knowing well that Bishop Azariah was a great Bishop indeed, Archdeacon P. B. Emmett, Deaconess Carol Graham, NCC Secretary J. Z. Hodge, G. V. Job and K. Hayberg have written their respective biographies of the Bishop. Studying the multifarious services and actions of a man renowned as the first Indian Anglican bishop, a great Indian Christian leader, and a global Christian Church scholar, and writing his complete biography is not an easy task.

At this time, when we celebrate the centenary of the founder and first Secretary of the Indian Missionary Society, and a peerless missionary, we publish this book, in which we have tried to portray him as a Missionary-Bishop of the Society.

A work of art created by a novice is bound to have shortcomings. Even if some shortcomings may appear in this book, to the extent that the God of Bishop Azariah has granted me the grace to write this book, I dedicate this book at the feet of Azariah's Lord and my Lord Jesus Christ.

A SHORT BIOGRAPHY OF REV. D.A.CHRISTADOSS

Rev. Devanesan Azariah Christadoss was born on 25th March 1912 to Rev. S.V. Devadasen and Thaiammal. To understand him better, one should first revisit his family legacy.

Rev. D.A. Christadoss's great grandparents were Narayana and Parvati, natives of Kovaikulam who became Christians in 1840. After baptism, Narayana became Gnanayutham and Parvathi became Packiam. Gnanayutham (Narayana) had two sons, the younger was Rev. D.A. Christadoss' grandfather, Vedamanickam. Vedamanickam had seminary training and married Ellen, a convert in 1857. Vedamanickam served as a catechist in Adaikalapuram from 1866 to 1876, and was ordained in 1876. After his ordination, he served as assistant pastor in Palayamkottai and later transferred to Parpillankulam in 1877. Unfortunately he died there of cholera in 1885, contracting the disease from an old woman parishioner, whom he had ministered the whole night, while others shied away in fear. Sadly, though he saved the old woman's life, he lost his own from the deadly disease. In those days, Cholera was a dreaded plague and people including several young British soldiers lost their lives. Many villages were deserted in panic. Rev. Vedamanickam was 50 years old when he died. After Rev. Vedamanickam's death, Bishop Sargent took his widow, Ellen, to Palayamkottai and appointed her as a Bible Woman.

Rev. Vedamanickam and Ellen had nine children, the eighth was Rev. D.A. Christadoss's father, Samuel Devadason.

Samuel Devadason went to Madras to be educated for ordained ministry and finished his Theological Course with high credit. He married Thaiammal, the youngest daughter of one of the most leading families in Palayamkottai. Rev. D.A. Christadoss grew up in Palayamkottai where he also worked as a court clerk. He met Emily Kamalam, the daughter of Rev. David Yesudian and Mary Thangammal, during a church meeting, where evangelist Sahayam was preaching. They married in 1936. Emily Kamalam was a medical doctor. They moved to Mudalur, the first Christian village in Tirunelveli District, where he worked as a Headmaster and there she ministered to the Christian community with a missionary zeal.

In 1942, encouraged by the Bishop, he joined Thirumaraiyoor Theological seminary, where he completed his theological studies and later his masters. He was asked to continue in Thirumaraiyoor Theological seminary as a Professor. However, in 1955, he shifted to Palayamkottai, where he became the Principal in Bishop Sargent Training School. Then in 1959, he moved to Serampore University, where he served as a Professor in Church History and later as the Bursar and Vice Principal of the University. While in Serampore, he also served for several years as the General Secretary of Church History Association of India. Then, unexpectedly a tragedy struck in the family. In 1964, his beloved wife Emily Kamalam died from hepatic amoebiasis, a liver infection, at the early age of 50 years and was buried there in Danish mission cemetery, near the Baptist Mission cemetery, where William Carey and William Ward, and Joshua Marshman the founders of Serampore College lay buried. Interestingly, William Ward died of cholera at Serampore on 7 March 1823.

Rev. D. A. Christadoss moved back to Tirunelveli diocese in 1972, and worked as a honourary pastor in Perumalpuram church, Palayamkottai. Later, he moved over to Bethel Agricultural Fellowship, Danishpet, Salem District, where his daughter, Dhamayanthi Jeyasingh was located and there he continued ministering, both as a teacher in Bethel Bible Institute and chaplain of the Fellowship, after which, he finally retired. He was 78 years old, when he died in the parsonage of St George's Church, Madurai, where his youngest son Sathiaraj Christadoss was ministering. Rev. D. A. Christadoss has written several books on church history and missions, particularly on Thirunelveli diocese. Research and writing was his only passion. He kept writing till his last breath. To his credit, he has mentored several theological students and helped them complete their theses. Many of his students have become Bishops and theological Professors. His entire library and writings, along with a cache of research books of Paul H. Jeyasingh, his son-in-law, have been donated to the Bishop Neil's Research Library, Palayamkottai, maintained by the Tirunelveli diocese. To our dismay, this much touted research library has been in disarray and neglect, because of lack of funds. However, in recent times, there seems to be some efforts by the management towards preservation and conservation of the books and rare manuscripts. In this context, we admire the initiatives taken by "**Tinnevelly Christian Historical Society**", Tirunelveli. They need all our support and encouragement.

Written and signed
by
Rev. D.A. Christadoss' children:
Mrs. Chandra Thomas (Malaysia)
Mr. Mathias Christadoss (Retd. Professor, Tanjavur)
Mrs. Leela Pandian (Retd. Headmistress, Chennai)
Mrs. Damayanthi Jeyasingh, Bangalore

Table of Contents

INTRODUCTION

Among the renowned missionary fathers who preached the redemption gospel of the Saviour Jesus and helped the Tirunelveli church grow was Rev. John Thomas! He was praised as the Apostle of South Tirunelveli. From 1837 to 1870, he made Meignanapuram, a hamlet, as his home. Around this hamlet, in an area covering a diameter of about 20 miles, he had the honor of establishing 70 Christian churches, and nurturing them. Out of the 70 churches, one still shines even today: the Vellalanvilai church. It was Rev. Thomas' custom to choose and admirably train Catechists in the churches that he established so that they, in turn, as ministers could nurture new Christians in Christian knowledge, devotion, and character. In this manner, he appointed Vedhanayagam Thomas, an upright man, as Catechist at Vellalanvilai. After serving as Catechist for ten years from 1858 to 1868, he served as pastor.

In a nearby hamlet lived a respected man who became wealthy by trading. He was a deeply religious Hindu. This man had a son called Velayudham. Somehow Velayudham heard the gospel of Christianity. He visited Rev. John Thomas to learn more about it. He became a believer and was baptized in 1839, and was given the name Vedhanayagam Thomas. Noticing Vedhanayagam's deep devotion and sharp mind,

Rev. Thomas gave him the needed training and appointed him as Catechist, as mentioned earlier. In due course, he appointed him as Catechist in Vellalanvilai. Vedhanayagam's heart was moved that he was afforded the opportunity to serve his Savior Jesus Christ. As a result, he worked diligently and carefully.

He chose to marry a woman who was equally devoted to God, and who would be an aid to his ministry. They had two sons, namely, Ambrose and Samuel Thomas. His family became a model of Christian family life, and won the respect and love of his congregation as well as the appreciation of missionaries. He received God's blessing in abundance, and he, in turn, became a blessing to many.

As he was serving the Vellalanvilai church as a faithful shepherd, he tried to get a church built there. His devotion, preaching skills and practical care of his flock in their adversity and prosperity won for him his people's abounding love, respect and deep appreciation. They listened to his counsel, whether they were for their earthly life or for their heavenly life. As a result, they received many good benefits.

Shortly after he started ministering in Vellalanvilai, Vedhanayagam's wife passed away. Having received great help from her in his church ministry, Vedhanayagam sank into inconsolable sorrow.

However, for the sake of the ministry and for the sake of bringing up his two little boys, he decided to get married again. He married a virtuous Christian woman called Helen. In course of time, she gave birth to a girl baby. They named her Johanna and brought her up uprightly and prosperously. Helen bore no children for many years thereafter.

During this time, a few missionaries and 17 Indian pastors served the fast-growing Tirunelveli CMS churches. Just eight pastors served the SPG churches. Therefore, it was decided to select some Catechists based on their skills, devotion to God and experience. They would be ordained as Assistant Pastors and, later, as Pastors. Accordingly, 15 Catechists from CMS churches and six Catechists from SPG churches were selected and ordained by the Chennai Bishop as Assistant Pastors.[1] Their ordination took place on January 18, 1869 at Holy Trinity Church in Palayamkottai. Vellalanvilai Catechist Vedhanayagam was one among those ordained, and he was the eldest among them and the most experienced too. Even after his ordination, he was not transferred to another place, but continued to serve in Vellalanvilai for 20 years. During the years 1869 to 1889, he served as Assistant Pastor for two years and as Pastor for eighteen years.

He served in the pastorate more vigorously than before. He was instrumental in starting many new churches and schools. He vigorously toiled in the construction of the church building in Vellalanvilai. In 1879, the building of this beautiful church was completed.

The pastor's elder son Ambrose became the Headmaster of a CMS School in Colombo (Sri Lanka). His younger son Thomas was educated in Meignanapuram and later in Tiruchi SPG College.

Helen felt that she was missing something because she had no son. The pastor knew his wife's grief. So, both of them began to pray to the Lord for a son. Helen prayed saying, "Lord, if you grant me a son, I will name him Samuel, and will bring him up consecrating him to your service, O God." God heard their prayer. Hearing the news, Vedhanayagam thanked the Lord. He was glad that if a son is born, his son would become a servant of God.

---

1. That day, eleven others were ordained as Pastors

On August 17, 1874, Helen's desire was fulfilled.[2] Though they already had a son named as Samuel, the parents christened their newborn son as Samuel Azariah, and got him baptized. They brought him up dedicating him to become a servant of God.

2.There is a history that once the elderly Bishop of Chennai Fredrick Gell met Helen and noticed that her face was sad because she grieved over the lack of a son. He turned to her and told her in a consoling and prophetic way, "Do not be sad. God will grant you a son." [From a speech Mr. J. Anbudaiyan delivered on August 6, 1920 at the Centenary Hall].

CHAPTER 1

THE BOY SAMUEL

"Speak, Lord, for your servant hears" I Samuel 3: 9.

"When I was yet a babe, my mother sanctified herself for my sake," said Bishop Azariah as he recalled it many years later. "My memory goes back to the days when, as a boy, I gradually began to understand things. The picture of my mother suddenly disappearing every now and then is still fresh in my mind. As a teary-eyed boy, I would look for her and find her deep in prayer in a room all alone."[1]

His father was busy with church affairs and pastorate work. In addition, he had to focus on the building project of the church. His elder brothers had moved out to other places. His elder sister was at Elliott Tuxford School in Meignanapuram. So, Samuel was always at home with his mother, who kept a watchful eye on little Samuel even as she was engaged in her household chores. Early in his life, when Samuel began to speak as a little child, his mother taught him short and simple Bible verses. Samuel never forgot those Bible verses that he had learned during that time.

His mother, who knew by experience that Prayer was her Life, often prayed kneeling down in a room of her small house. Little Samuel, who looked for her and found her praying, could not understand why she was doing this. In course of time, when he understood it, he asked his mother,

1. From an address delivered by Bishop Azariah at the Mothers' Union Conference at Christchurch, New Zealand, 1923.

"Why should we pray often?" "My son, God gave you to us in answer to our prayers," said the saintly lady. "Your father and I have already dedicated you for God's service. So, should I not seek in prayer God's guidance to bring you up in accordance with your calling?" Later, whenever Bishop Azariah recalled this scene in his life, his heart would melt in thankfulness to God, and he would exclaim, "My mother sanctified herself for my sake!"

While recalling a valuable truth that his mother planted in his heart in his boyhood days, Bishop Azariah said: "My mother used to often emphasize that a human being's relationship with God was higher than any other relationship."[2] Not only did Samuel keep this truth in his heart all through his life, but also put it into practice.

Once he went to Dornakal as a missionary, and his mother wrote him a letter expressing her grief that he was so far away from her. The bishop replied in a letter to her: "I do not feel like I suffer from self-despair because I left Tirunelveli to be engaged in this work. Your self-despair is great too.... However, for the sake of the Lord's ministry, and because you have dedicated me for His service, God will accordingly grant you His peace and blessing. Just as you feel sad that you are separated from me, I also feel sad that I am separated from you. It is God's will that we, who know the love of God (Who gave His Son for us not even considering that He is His own Son), should be separated for His sake and the gospel's sake. At the right time, may the same God grant us the privilege of meeting each other and praising Him."[3]

The first letter that Samuel Azariah wrote to his wife soon after their marriage provides additional evidence that he religiously followed the truth that his mother had taught him. A few weeks after his marriage, he had to tour Kerala to fulfill his duties as YMCA Secretary. The young couple

2. ibid.

3. A Tamil letter to his mother, dated August 2, 1909.

started feeling the pain of separation. His wife requested him to postpone the trip. But the duty-conscious Azariah could not comply with her request, but departed on the due date. His wife bid farewell to him with tears. No sooner than he reached Trichur, he wrote a letter to her, stating: "My darling, how cruel is separation! It gives the same kind of agony as soul's departure gives. But, it's for Him! (let's rejoice in this)…"[4]

Some months later, they had to be separated again. Recalling the sorrow she felt at their last separation, this time he consoled her by writing: "Separation causes deep distress. It's a fact. Is it not wrong to give place to sorrow when we are at the place that God has appointed for us to be that day? Rev. H. J. Schaffter used to say, 'sorrow comes when we oppose the will of God'. But we have not stood against God's will. How, then, can we give place to sorrow and worry?"[5]

"A human being's relationship with God is far higher than all kinds of relationships that human beings have with one another." His mother who taught him this truth also taught him another good quality. Even from a young age, she taught him to love his Lord. Samuel Azariah not only learned to love his Lord from a young age, but also learned to love the Lord's ministry. Unawares, he began to nurture an intensive desire that all ought to know and love the Lord as he did. At that young age, what triggered abounding joy in him was his parents' narration of missionary histories.

When he was about eleven years old, he joined Meignanapuram Boarding School for his education. In those times, King Mwanga of Uganda persecuted Christians. Many died as martyrs. Especially, the then Christian world marveled at the strong faith of three boys. One day a missionary was narrating the history of how the church in Uganda began and grew. He narrated in detail how despite the trouble caused by

4. Letter to his wife, dated August 6, 1898.

5. Letter dated February 13, 1899.

Mwanga, many martyrs including Bishop Hanington displayed courage and faced death with valor. These narrations broke Samuel's heart. His eyes shed tears. When offering was taken for the ministry in Uganda and for the suffering Christians, 'little Samuel, the prophet', took the silver bracelets adorning his hands, which his parents had lovingly given him to wear, and put these in 'the collection bag' that ushers held before him. Were his parents angry at this? Did his mother cry out in grief? No, not at all! On the contrary, they praised God on seeing the light of 'Christian charity' burn bright in their beloved son's heart.

This passion for missionary ministry' never departed from his heart. His mother was very concerned that his desire for winning souls should stay alive in his young heart. In later days, his father-in-law also wished that in no circumstances should his son-in-law leave God's ministry in which the latter was directly involved, even though the salary of a minister was meager. Earlier, we saw that soon after his marriage, Azariah left for Trichur in Kerala to do his YMCA ministry. While he stayed in Trichur, the President of the Administrative Committee of a local High School persuaded Azariah to accept the position of Mathematics teacher at his school. At the same time, he also offered to Azariah's wife the position of Headmistress of the local Girls School. Both Azariah and his wife would have well-paid jobs. The salary appeared attractive. The town was good. Shall we accept it? That was the question. He wrote elaborately in a long letter to his wife describing the job offer:

"Shall we move to Trichur? It's a fine and healthy place. I think we should come here. But our parents[6] would quarrel with us. So, let's leave it."[7]

It is evident from this letter that Azariah's mother, who had with love and consideration named him as 'Samuel',

6. Azariah used to address his father-in-law as 'Dad'. His wife used to address mother-in-law as 'Mom'.

7. Letter dated August 8, 1898.

was steadfast in her resolve that her son should not even slightly stray from the Lord's work. She did not deviate from her resolution from his childhood through his youth and his married life.

One of the main purposes of missionaies starting Boarding Schools was that the children of pastors and catechists would be educated in these schools so that they would eventually qualify for missionary service. Most students who studied in CMS Boarding Schools in such places as Palayamkottai, Meignanapuram, Nallur, Surandai and Pannaivilai fell in this category. Moreover, village schools had classes only up to Grade III. Missionaries considered that the children of those serving God should complete their higher studies too.

After completing his studies up to Grade III in the village school at Vellalanvilai, Samuel Azariah joined the Boarding School at Meignanapuram. 'The child Samuel' did not give up the good Christian virtues that he had imbibed from his parents from his childhood. He did not lose his living faith in his Lord, fear of God, love and such virtues. 'The child Samuel' was known in school as a boy of excellent character. (It was at this time that he had donated his silver bracelets for the ministry in Uganda, as we saw earlier).

However, it is normal for children growing into adulthood to exhibit changes in their behavior. Some changes may be welcome changes; others may be undesirable changes. Among them are boyhood pranks. His loving mother never hesitated to use the cane to punish in order to get rid of such boyhood pranks, especially when the pranks were undesirable and could badly influence his devotional life. So, Samuel greatly feared his mother's strictness. The little boy used to imagine how much he might have hurt his mother's heart that she, with her love-filled heart, wanted to punish him. The boy realized that his mother's caning caused a little pain here and there in his body, but the pain in his mother's heart in caning him was greater! After such realization, would he ever cause heartache to his mother again? He immediately gave up whatever prank or action of his that had pained his mother. He also learned to be careful not to repeat such mistakes in the future.

Meignanapuram Boarding School was close to the local church. It had taken many years to construct the church building. It was dedicated on January 22, 1885. Traditionally, Saint Paul's conversion day is observed on January 25. Therefore, the church was called St. Paul's Church. Multitudes of Christians from the surrounding villages assembled there for the dedication festival of the church building. Rev. Vedhanayagam and his family, along with members of his church, attended the dedication festival. After the dedication was over, Samuel's parents got young Samuel admitted in the Boarding School, and they returned to Vellalanvilai.

At the Boarding School, the boys had to do many tasks. They had to keep the school rooms and its precincts clean by sweeping the place. Secondly, they had to help in the kitchen. They had to do many such tasks. They had to water the flowering plants and the fruit-yielding trees. One day, some of the boys who were watering the plants, climbed the trees and stole some fruits, and ate them. Little Samuel was with the boys on the ground. The garden was under the care of the wife of Rev. Thomas Sr., who nurtured the garden. She kept an account of the number of ripe fruits, raw fruits and buds in each and every branch of every tree. She also kept an account of the number of flowers and flowering buds in each plant.

As was her custom, one morning she went around the garden and noticed some fruits missing. She assumed that the boys who had watered the tree the previous evening must have stolen the fruits. She ordered the boys to see her. The boys came and stood in a line. Mrs. Thomas was a compassionate woman. She wept when she saw people suffer. She thought it is better to make the boys realize their offence than to punish them for it. "What does the Bible say about thieves?" she questioned. "Today, you shall be with me in paradise," was the prompt, mischievous reply from a boy. She got angry. "Punishment is not only for those who stole the fruits, but also for those who ate them", she said. "Stretch out your hands," she ordered, with a cane in her hand. The cane fell on every stretched hand. The last hand was Samuel's. As she raised her hand to cane him, her hand stopped midway. Did she hesitate because it was the hand of a 13 year old boy? Was she confused whether or not to cane the hand that had donated the silver bracelets? Was she astonished that he was the pastor's son? No! She felt that his mother's punishment out of love would have the desired effect on him than she beating him. "Samuel, I will not cane you" she said. "I will report the matter to your mother". Tears welled up in Samuel's eyes. "She will report it to my mother", Samuel thought to himself. "How much it would pain my mother's heart when she hears that I stole the fruit or was in the company of the boys who stole the fruits or that I ate a stolen fruit! What shall I do? Mother will beat me." "Madam, please beat me," he said to Mrs. Thomas. "I can't bear my mother's beating." She caned Samuel's outstretched hand as she caned the other boys.

One of the school teachers was Samuel's elder brother Ambrose. After returning from Colombo in 1882, Ambrose joined Meignanapuram School as a teacher. The Headmaster of the school was Abraham David. The school had classes up to Grade VI only. In appreciation of Ambrose's knowledge and experience, higher officials assigned him the position of Class Teacher of Grade VI, while assigning the Headmaster as Class Teacher of Grade V. Samuel passed out from both these classes. In 1887, when the school was upgraded as Middle School, and classes for Grade VII were started, Samuel studied under his elder brother Ambrose who was the teacher for that Grade. The following year, the school was upgraded to High School. That year, the school Headmaster David retired, and Ambrose became the Headmaster. He took classes for Grades IV, V and VI, all in one year, and in the year 1888, he, to his credit, made some students appear for the final Matriculation School examination. The next year too, Ambrose did this.[8] His younger brother Azariah Samuel was one of the students who appeared for the Matriculation examination in 1889. Samuel was 15 years old at that time.

Meanwhile, on June 23, 1889, at the age of 68, Samuel's father Vedhanayagam passed away. He had served as Catechist and Pastor for 32 years from 1858 to 1889 in Vellalanvilai[9]. As an upright shepherd, an eminent believer, excellent saint and good preacher, he won people's appreciation, love and respect. He succeeded in turning Vellalanvilai as 'a model Christian village'. He also succeeded in nurturing the local Christian church in devotion to God and Christian character. Members of the Vellalanvilai pastorate grieved that they lost their upright shepherd. Helen fell into grief over her departed husband, and Samuel sorrowed inconsolably for losing his loving father.

"Whatever happens, we should submit to God's compassionate will, and we should ensure that no human relationship affects our relationship with God." Having made this truth as the motto of their lives, both mother and son were comforted in course of time, and began to fulfill their God-given duties.

Earlier, we noticed that Samuel passed his Matriculation examination with flying colors, even though he had to study the lessons / syllabi of three years in just one year. Despite the pain he experienced on the loss of his father, he succeeded well academically. This shows that he fulfilled his duties paying serious attention to them.

---

8. "Rev. Ambrose V. Thomas", a Pamphlet by P. V. Jesudason, page 1.
9. Bishop Azariah also served for 32 years.

His mother worked as a Matron at the Girls School in Meignanapuram. We may say that Samuel's success in his examinations to some extent consoled his mother who had lost her husband.

The next two years, Samuel joined C. M. College in Tirunelveli town for his F. A. Degree. The senior Rev. Schaffter's younger son Henry Schaffter was the Principal of the college. He was an excellent saint. He was greatly cconcerned about the spiritual matters of his students.

Beinga wareof Samuel'sdevotiontoGod,heencouraged Samuel by assigning to him several responsibilities in the college student community. By discharging the duties given to him in an excellent manner, Samuel won the Principal's love and goodwill. At the same time, he profusely earned the friendship and regards of his fellow-students.

His love for the Lord constrained him to lead many nominal Christians to redemption, and to be a suitable guide for them to lead a reformed life. He had influence over students of other faiths too.

Many of the students hailed from villages. Staying in the college hostel, they did their studies. Samuel also stayed in the hostel. In those days, Christian students showed interest in gospel ministry. One of the aims of Rev. Schaffter when he established the hostel in 1883 was to nurture Christian characteristics in Christian students so that they may evangelize high caste people[10].* Particularly, his aim was to spread the Christian influence among high caste Hindus.

In the beginning, these aims were fulfilled well. Every year, at least a few Brahmin boys became Christians and were

10. Letters of H. J. Schaffter to Home Boards and other Committees, 1880s and 1990s.

baptized.

However, when Samuel joined the college, the hostel students had lost their spiritual warmth. In addition, after Bishop Sergeant's death, changes were effected in the administrative structure of Tirunelveli C. M. S. This led to competitive mindset among the leaders. And this triggered caste discord. Christians were differentiated as 'Vellala Christians', 'Nadar Christians', 'Maravar Christians' and so on, based on their castes. Christian brotherhood, love and fellowship weakened. This malady spread to the C. M. Hostel too. It pained the hearts of some students like Samuel who were devoted to God and displayed virtuous Christian character.

Therefore, they began to gather for prayers. They prayed to God in tears. "Lord, please abolish this evil," they said as they poured out their grievances to God. "What do you want us to do?" they asked God. And they waited for an answer from God.

They received God's guidance. Samuel started a group called 'the Christian Brotherhood' comprising students of various castes, who were already praying with him. In order to develop their own personal spiritual life, members of the group engaged themselves in Bible study, meditation and prayer. Apart from getting involved in these, they developed their own conduct and character. At the same time, they spread Christian brotherhood and loving fellowship, considering these as their own paramount duty. The group ran a magazine called 'Living Water', which was pulsating in faith. In our considered opinion those who knew that this group published the magazine also knew that many of its readers, who knew what they experienced by reading it and reaped its benefits, would have not forgotten it.

Several younger missionaries of those times deeply desired that the college should be upgraded to the Undergraduate level. But some experienced persons like Schaffter and Camper did not like this idea. "Tirunelveli Hindu College would be upgraded, and C. M. College would lag behind," said some. With this kind of reasoning, they expected Schaffter to comply with their request. But Schaffter did not budge. As a result, those who wanted to pursue their undergraduate degree (Bachelor of Arts) had to move to Tiruchi or Chennai.

In 1891, Samuel passed his F. A. examinations. There was a rumor that Hindu College was starting B. A. degree course the following year. Rev. Schaffter had gone on furlough to England during this time. At once Rev. Ardill wrote to Schaffter that at least now he should give up his obstinacy and agree to start B. A. degree classes in our college. He also emphatically requested Schaffter to return to India[11]. But it was of no avail.

To study in Madras Christian College in Chennai would prove to be an expensive affair. Samuel's mother, who now worked as a Matron at the Meignanapuram Girls School, could not afford to send her son to pursue his undergraduate degree (B. A.) studies. The son, however, deeply desired to go for his undergraduate degree (B. A.) studies. What to do? Mother and son prayed together. They concluded that Samuel would work for a year and save enough money to pursue his bachelor's degree the following year. His mother also would save some money and chip in. This way it would be possible for Samuel to pursue his Bachelor's degree the following year in Chennai.

Today's Saint John's College and Cathedral High School were in those days known as Palayamkottai CMS Higher Education centre.This centre was in the South Campus[12]. Mr. Edwin Keyworth was its Principal. The school also had a Boarding House.

Samuel approached Keyworth for a job. Keyworth

11. Letter of Rev. R. F. Ardill to Rev. H. J. Schaffter, dated November 14, 1891

12. The campus where Bishop Sergeant Teachers school is located today.

already knew Samuel. Therefore, in February 1892, Keyworth appointed Samuel as Monitor to assist the Hostel Warden and other teachers. The position was called 'Master'. Samuel lived in a room in the Hostel, and supervised students' Bible-reading, academic studies, mess (food) affairs, etc. He also resolved quarrels and fights among the students. In this way, he proved to be a great boon to the manager and teachers. In addition, he began to prepare himself for the forthcoming B. A. degree examinations. Thus he began his preparations for the Chennai college life.

In February of the following year, he was admitted to the B. A. degree course at Madras Christian College. When he resigned from his job at Palayamkottai CMS School, the school's Manager and Principal Edwin Keyworth gave him a Certificate. It indicated even then some of the primordial characteristics of a bishop in Samuel.

January 20, 1893 CMS High School

Palayamkottai.

Azariah V. Samuel worked as a Monitor in our School from last February. I happily endorse his zeal, goodness, ability and industry. These served us well. He was affectionate and firm with the students. He himself resolved their quarrels and fights without taking them to other teachers.

By passing the distinguished Peter Cater Bible examination and by preparing for his B. A. examinations, he set an excellent example. Now he is leaving us for his B. A. studies. He has a passion to serve as a Sunday school teacher.

Edwin
Keyworth
Manager & Principal

Samuel joined B. A. degree classes at Madras Christian College, Chennai. He chose Mathematics as his main subject. The renowned scholar Rev. Arthur Miller was its Principal. Among the other professors, noteworthy scholars were Cooper and Skinner. They held the foremost place in the then educational world.

The day he joined the college, Miller asked Samuel, "What's your name?"

"Samuel," he replied.

"Samuel, there are many here who bear the name Samuel; do you have any other name?" asked Miller.

"Yes, Sir, I also bear my father's name Vedhanayagam," said Samuel.

The Principal found it hard to pronounce that name. So he proclaimed: "It's a long name. Any other name, please?"

"Yes, Sir, it's Azariah," Samuel replied.

"Well, that's a good name! Here we'll call you Azariah," said Miller.

"That's fine, Sir," said Samuel in acceptance of Miller's suggestion. Since then Samuel was known as "V. S. Azariah" for "Vedhanayagam Samuel Azariah".

Just as he was an excellent student at the Tirunelveli C. M. College, at the college in Chennai too, he was an excellent student. He won accolades from all teachers, particularly from Miller. His fellow students respected him and listened to him. He made valuable friends there. He learned several good things from his college life.

Examination days came. He looked forward to those days expectantly because he was well prepared. But after appearing for one or two examinations, he was down with fever. The fever became severe. He could not appear for the examinations in the remaining subjects. What a pity! Azariah was very disappointed. Miller and the other professors grieved that Azariah, who could have brought laurels for himself and the college by passing the examinations in flying colors, could not appear for the examinations.

Azariah comforted himself that he could pass the examinations the following year, and obtain his B. A. degree.

But the following year too he fell sick with fever, and could not appear for his examinations. He grieved on account of this. His mother's sorrow was indescribable because she had sacrificed herself to get her son educated. Azariah, however, thought deeply over it and concluded that the same obstacle twice prevented him from appearing for his degree examinations.

He felt it was God's will. If so, his God was willing to lead him in some way, according to His will. This thought comforted him. As soon he was healed, he returned to his village.

His mother welcomed him with joy. One day, in her conversation with him, she happened to say how disappointed she was that he could not succeed in the degree examinations. She wished that her son would appear for the examinations once again. Azariah's mind was against it. His mother began to compel him. "Mother, having dedicated me for God's ministry even before I was born, should you sorrow so much for my losing this worldly pride?" asked Azariah finally, thus putting an end to their conversation.

Since then, his mother never again bothered about it. He also forgot about it.

Nevertheless, all his life Azariah did not forget the rare privileges he got from his life at Madras Christian College, the scholar Miller's advice, and how Miller bid farewell to him and his fellow students, committing them all to God's protection and leading.

CHAPTER 2
THE MAN AZARIAH

"The Spirit of God came upon Azariah" II Chronicles 15: 1

After he finished his studies at the Chennai college, Azariah tried to find a job. While at college from 1893 to 1895, he had become a member of the Young Men's Christian Association (YMCA) and had engaged actively in their services. He reaped many spiritual benefits by regularly attending their Bible Study classes and devotional meetings. The Association offered Christian fellowship, friendship, exchange of ideas, and opportunities to do voluntary service. These helped him develop his personality. For these reasons, he developed an interest in the Association. The YMCA President Mr. David McConaugby got to know about Azariah.

When Azariah expressed to Mr. McConaugby his desire to work for YMCA, McConaugby gladly received him and appointed him in March 1895 as 'Assistant Secretary' at the Chennai branch. Azariah was pleased to accept his appointment, and left for Chennai. He got involved in his job with full enthusiasm. He rejoiced that God accepted him who had been dedicated for the Lord's ministry. He resolved in himself to render the work given to him as if he was serving the Lord himself. With this determination, he fulfilled his duties carefully and in humility and with a sense of gratitude. Daily he prayed to God that the Holy Spirit's strength may be perfected in him who was weak. Thus he discharged his duties.

He did not forget the good habits that he had learned

from his mother. Rising up early in the morning, he would meditate on the Holy Scriptures and then pray for a long time upon his knees. Only after this would he perform his other duties. It was during this time that he learned by experience the Christian truth that one can obtain more power by praying for others than by praying for one's own self[1]. After getting to know this truth, he started praying daily morning and evening for the many young people he had come to know through the Chennai city YMCA, and for the students at Madras Christian College, and for others. His prayers began to bear fruit. Many young people surrendered their lives to the Lord and began to live transformed Christian lives.

The desire Azariah had from his young age that others should experience 'the peace and joy in Christ' that he had experienced, now turned into strong passion. Therefore, he began to work tirelessly among Christian youth and students. He brought together the students who had already repented and begun a new life so that he may register in their hearts the need to propagate the gospel of Lord Jesus. He also taught them how to accomplish the work of proclaiming the gospel. He got them involved in practicing what they had learned. Whenever he proclaimed the gospel to people of other faiths, he took along the students whom he had trained so that they may also proclaim the gospel. He made this ministry which he did 'directly' to the Lord as his life-goal. Yet, he did not consider it as arising from his own enthusiasm and efforts. He firmly believed "the call to ministry comes from the God of grace; and we have to realize that we are in no way qualified to do ministry and that we are unfit to do it. The merciful God grants us this calling in order that we may, through prayer and quiet waiting, struggle to receive the 'sanctification' and strength needed for the ministry."[2]

1. "V. S. Azariah - An Appreciation" by G. S. Eddy, 1909.

2. Quoted by Deaconess Carol Graham in her "Azariah of Dornakal", page 10.

After a year, YMCA higher authorities promoted him to the position of 'Regional Secretary' and ordered him to function as South India secretary based in Madurai. He was just twenty one and half years old at that time. Trusting in the strength that God grants, he boldly accepted this great responsibility and in 1896 he moved to Madurai, and engaged himself in the ministry. In this job, he had to work industriously visiting various places and meeting those at the YMCA branches. He began to motivate them. He also established branches in places where no branch existed. Though he was just about 22, he made the branch secretaries brace themselves for their work by encouraging them. He provided help to those who needed help. Thus Azariah obtained their love and respect by remaining a good friend and a sympathetic higher official to them. College principals did not look down upon him because of his tender age. His sweet talk that voiced his fear of God as well as his enthusiasm for soul-winning attracted them to him. They provided him many opportunities and facilities to conduct meetings in their colleges, where they called students to repentance and offered sound advice that would benefit their spiritual life. They also started Bible classes and strengthened existing Christian student groups.

When he was thus fulfilling his duties without rest, pastors from Tamilnadu began to give him work. Having observed his remarkable work among the youth, they began to invite him to help them in strengthening the spiritual life of their church members, catechists, teachers and church ministers by conducting spiritual meetings for them.

They also invited him to spiritually revitalize their catechists serving in their areas as well as teachers, church ministers and members of their church. Azariah did not think that he was too young to minister to church ministers who generally were older and more experienced than him. Nor was he shy that pastors may attend his meetings. He did not consider his ministry to be an impediment to his YMCA job. He did not entertain such thoughts, but worked tirelessly and vigorously by giving the Lord's message wherever he had the opportunities. "Pastors in scattered villages, catechists, voluntary workers who heard this spiritual teacher would remember for long time the words that he spoke. Azariah's words were a blessing to them. They felt new joy in their Christian ministry. His words helped them draw closer to God."[3]

Having started this kind of ministry in 1896, Azariah had to visit Kolkata one day. There he had the opportunity to meet the young American missionary George Sherwood Eddy, who became his life-long comrade and upright friend. Azariah was the first Indian whom Sherwood met as soon as he landed in India. Their meeting was like the confluence of two wild streams rushing towards each other. Azariah's heart and Eddy's heart were like two wild streams stirred up by the Holy Spirit for His work. Both their hearts were constrained by the love of Christ. No sooner than they met, they became friends. Their love for the Lord united them.

Having been appointed as the Travelling Secretary for the YMCA in India and Sri Lanka, Eddy arrived in India. He was deeply devoted to God. He was like Azariah in his passion for the gospel work. Eddy too had made soul-winning as the goal of his life. No wonder then that they became close friends.

It was during this time that Azariah got introduced to Rev. John Raleigh Mott, and they became friends. Mott was the pioneer in global unity. Mott founded the Student Volunteer Movement for Foreign Missions, D. L. Moody being its initial force. Even before he became a Bishop, Azariah became known to the world through Mott.

During this time, Azariah became dear to his Indian friends K. T. Paul (who later became a leader), S. K. Dutta, P. C. Sircar, and in Tirunelveli S. G. Madhuram, S. Paramanandham, D. S. David and J. Anbudaiyan.

3. Eddy – Op. cit.

His mother was proud of her son Azariah when she heard all about him through letter correspondence. On the one hand she was happy to know that her son was engaged "in God's work, in the business of winning souls, and kept himself busy in his ministry work". On the other hand, she despaired that there was none to welcome him home when he returned after a hard day's work. There was nobody to console him with a loving face. She was sad that he had to cook his own meals. She worried that there was no one to take care of him if he fell sick. In short, she concluded that the time had come for him to have a wife to take care of him.

Azariah knew his mother's desire, but God's time should come!

Mothers of prospective brides approached his mother. About fifty years ago, an evil custom started breeding among much of the Christian society in Tirunelveli. According to this evil custom, eligible bachelors with eminent qualifications such as 'an educated boy, a pastor's son holding a job at the YMCA' commanded a high price in the marriage market. Therefore, many parents came forward offering cash and gold jewelry as dowry for their prospective son-in-law. Knowing her son's character, the mother realized that he longed neither for gold nor for cash as dowry. Alas! Her concern now was whether he will agree to marry or not!

However, Azariah had certain expectations about his marriage. The prospective bride should hold high educational qualification. She must be known as a virtuous woman. Above all, she must be a God-fearing woman. Azariah loathed behaviors such as ostentation, pomp, boasting and selfishness. Therefore, he wished to marry a simple girl. He hated business-like talk of gold jewelry and cash as dowry in marriage. His mother knew his mindset. Therefore, she waited patiently for his wholehearted consent.

The year 1884, Sarah Tucker Girls School re-opened after vacation. Mrs. Rebecca worked as a teacher in one of the branch schools of Sara Tucker School. Rebecca admitted her little daughter Anbu Maria in Grade IV at the branch school in Tirunelveli.

The fair-complexioned little girl was naturally intelligent, well-behaved, God-fearing and of a good character.

Mrs. Rebecca hailed from Kongarayakurichi. After completing her primary school education at the CMS School there, she continued her education at Sarah Tucker Girls School. After finishing her school education, she underwent Teachers' Training course there. Then she took up a job as a teacher at the Kongarayakurichi School.

There was a man in Pudhukudi near Srivaikundam who had recently received Christ. His name was Samuel. He trained at the Catechists Training School in Tirunelveli. He worked as Jones Band Catechist and preacher in Pannaivilai. It was then that he got married to Rebecca.

To Samuel and Rebecca was born their first child, a daughter, whom they named Anbu Maria. Thereafter Rebecca gave birth to their son Moses Sreenivasagam. All other children born to them died at a tender age.

It was Rev. A. H. Lash, the then Manager and Administrator of Sarah Tucker School, who established many branch schools in places where CMS churches existed. He had established three schools in Tirunelveli. In 1876, he opened a fourth school there. This school did not flourish. He determined that one of his former students Rebecca can revive and run this school. So, in 1884, he appointed Rebecca as Teacher.

Neither the present-day Bookshop under the Bishop's

control nor the earlier Diocesan Book Depot existed at that time. In 1883, Bibles were sold at the CMS Reading Room in Tirunelveli. When they appointed Rebecca as a teacher at a branch school in Tirunelveli, they also appointed preacher Samuel as Colporteur. From 1884, it was so arranged that he had to oversee the Reading Room as well as Bible distribution.

Consequently, Samuel and Rebecca with their children, moved to Tirunelveli. They raised their children with love and strictness, inculcating in them the fear of God and Christian character.

In her lifestyle, attitude, modesty, passion for church, looking after others' welfare, and in her good works, and in many other ways, she set a good example to other women. She also fulfilled her responsibilities as a school teacher faithfully, uprightly, and with a good conscience. She performed her duties wholeheartedly and with all her strength as unto the Lord. Her family was poor. Apart from her household chores, she had to raise her little children amidst their pranks. Being weak herself, she found all such things burdensome. She had to face many miseries. Despite all her circumstances, she bore a smiling face and radiance in her countenance. Her cheerfulness encouraged others. Her eyes never showed weariness. Thus she proved to be an upright wife to her husband and kept her husband happy always.[4]

Therefore, it is no wonder then that her daughter Anbu Maria also imbibed all her mother's good nature. Realizing the hardships faced by her parents, Maria with great concern focused on her studies and passed her school examinations every year. Her integrity, virtues, God-fearing nature, love (her name Anbu means 'love'), humility, modesty, soft talk, etc won the appreciation of her school teachers, and especially that of her school Principal Anne Jane Askwith.

---

4. Narpothagam (Good Teachings), April 1892.

After passing her Matriculation School examinations in 1890-91, Anbu enrolled herself in the Teachers' Training school. However, it doesn't seem that she completed this course. On 18th February 1892, while teaching in her school at Tirunelveli, Rebecca suddenly died of 'obstructive gas' formation. She was buried the same evening at Adaikalapuram Cemetery in Palayamkottai.[5] On the one side, Anbu grieved over the sudden death of her mother. On the other side, as the eldest child in the family, the burden of taking care of her younger sisters, her father and her 5-year old youngest brother Abraham fell upon her. We think that owing to this twin distress she could not appear for her examinations.

Although Anbu Maria could not obtain the Teachers' Training certificate, Madam Askwith, who knew Anbu's skills and appreciated them, appointed her during 1893-96 as teacher to teach in Forms II and III at her school.

Madam Askwith, with her comrade and fellow-minister Madam Florence Swainson, attempted to merge the Blind School, the Deaf & Dumb Class, and the Nurses' Training Class with the Sarah Tucker School but met with little success. Their goal was to turn Sarah Tucker establishment into a 'Women's Medical College'. However, CMS missionaries, especially retired Rev. A. H. Lash (former Manager of Sarah Tucker School) and Rev. Harcourt, strongly objected to their plans. Consequently, the Blind School moved to the High Grounds, and the Deaf & Dumb class had to be shut down. Later, Madam Florence Swainson, with her personal efforts, moved the Deaf & Dumb class to Koolavaanigapuram, and revived it there. By 1890, their dreams of opening Nurses Training class and a medical college were dashed.

Some years later, Madam Askwith, who had taken personal efforts to develop Sarah Tucker Girls School into a

5. Register of Burials, Tinnevelly.

High School, now set her eyes on it to upgrade it to a college to conduct F. A. classes. For this, she obtained the approval of the CMS headquarters. A new building was also raised. At the same time, a church building also was built. In the same year, F. A. classes started. In 1896, it blossomed into Sarah Tucker College.

One of the earliest students at this college was Anbu Maria. Her desire was to quit her teaching profession and pursue higher education. Madam Askwith gave Anbu her blessing. Anbu studied with great enthusiasm and obtained her F. A. certificate which was then the highest certificate girls could obtain in South India.

As he was completing his college studies, in January 1898, Azariah's eyes fell upon the virtuous Anbu Maria, whom God was going to givehim as his life partner. On seeing her, certain thoughts began to arise in his heart.

From 1897, Azariah resided in Palayamkottai. His mother was happy that her son had moved from faraway Madurai to nearby Palayamkottai. Palayamkottai was the headquarters of the CMS ministry. In Palayamkottai, there were many Boys Schools and Girls Schools, two colleges, a Printing Press and a Bookshop. Apart from this, there was a YMCA branch that was being run efficiently. This branch was established in 1891 in the CMS High School campus by Rev. John Barton. The head of the school Rev. Keyworth strengthened that branch by making many of his school students as its members. Almost all teachers became its members. Missionaries such as E. S. Carr, T. Walker and E. A. Douglas as well as Indian church pastors became its members and got it involved in various ministries like Bible studies, Vacation Bible School and Evangelistic ministry. From the time Azariah started residing in Palayamkottai, the branch multiplied its services and worked with great enthusiasm.

Often, the three friends Azariah, Madhuram and Paramanandham conducted spiritual meetings starting from Tirunelveli and visiting many towns and cities, thus helping many to prosper their souls. Missionaries like Carr, Walker, Camper and Shaffter motivated and encouraged them in this ministry.

From June 24-27, 1897, Sherwood Eddy conducted a "YMCA Mission Conference" at CMS School in Palayamkotai. In that meeting, it was considered on how to further extend the ministry. Because Palayamkottai YMCA had close connection with CMS schools, the city youth could not get involved in it. So, the CMS School YMCA branch was divided into three sub-divisions: 1. CMS High School branch; 2. CMS Teachers Training School branch; 3. Tirunelveli city branch. Azariah assisted the three branches to grow individually. At times, he also operated them in unison.

About six months earlier, in December 1896, in league with American saints John R. Mott, founder of the Student Voluntary Movement for Foreign Missions, his associate minister Robert Wilder, Campbell White and others, Azariah had conducted an "All India College Students Conference" in Chennai city. As head of the C. M. College Rev. Schaffter was on furlough at that time, its ad hoc head Rev. Douglas and Azariah along with some students attended the conference. John Mott conducted Bible Studies motivating the participants to grow in holiness. Robert Wilder emphasized the need for being filled by the Holy Spirit. Campbell White spoke poignantly on the need for Student Volunteers in order to win India for Christ. Multitudes of students from 40 colleges across India attended the conference. Out of them, 170 participants vowed to wake up early every morning to spend time in prayer and waiting upon the Lord (Morning Watch). They also surrendered their lives to God. Further, forty one persons made a solemn declaration stating that they will do life-long evangelistic work.[6] Azariah

6. Annual Report, 1896, to the CMS from E. A. Douglas, dated December

and Eddy gave necessary advice to these students so that they could stay firm in their determinations.

Azariah and his close friend Professor J. Anbudaiyan of C. M. College accomplished the 'follow-up work' at their college in an excellent manner. As a result of that, a YMCA branch was started in C. M. College.[7]

In the latter part of the year 1897, Azariah and Eddy traveled all over the states of Tamilnadu and Kerala, and established new YMCA branches in various places. They also held spiritual meetings. Many students took 'the Morning Watch' vow in those places. They began to live transformed lives.

In the beginning of the following year, Azariah began to think about his marriage. He enquired about the damsel whom he had seen one day wondering whether she was the one who would be a suitable life partner to him. He made himself certain that Anbu Maria was the girl after his own heart in her education, God-fearing nature and her character. The girl's family was a large one. Her father was a poor colporteur, that is, bookseller. Because of his meager income the family suffered under poverty. The girl was a gem. Although she was poor as far as worldly assets were concerned, in being 'poor in spirit' she belonged to nobility. Once it was clear that the Lord was showing him the colporteur Samuel's daughter to be his life-partner, Azariah sought his mother's permission.
Having waited wondering when her son would seek her permission. to marry a girl, Azariah's mother immediately gave her consent.

In keeping with the custom, the bridegroom's family sent word to the girl's family seeking the girl's hand in marriage. The girl's father was amazed. Azariah was a YMCA secretary.

1896.
7. ibid.

He had a good job. His family belonged to the creamy layer of the society. He had contacts with great people. "He is seeking my daughter's hand," thought Anbu's father. "Moreover, he has refused gold jewelry or cash as dowry. He does not want a grand wedding. He refuses to have music band perform at his wedding. Nor does he want expensive clothes. Simple clothes and feast for the poor too – these are enough for his wedding. What prevents them from giving their daughter to Azariah? How would the girl's attitude be?"

When they asked their daughter, she did not answer lightly. She did not have the courage to say 'yes' to this offer without first praying and ensuring that it was God's will. Oh! She is Madam Rebecca's daughter! Days rolled by. There were many doubts in the heart of this naïve girl.What is his nature? Is he a short-tempered man or a meek man? Does he have a loving heart or is he a man who will have no interest in me or concern for me?

In this manner, thoughts began to race in her mind. Finally, on February 15, Anbu gave her consent to marry Azariah. Many years later, Azariah would recall in a letter that February 15 was a special day for him rather than August 17.

The betrothal of Azariah and Anbu took place on March 23. After his betrothal, Azariah left for Meignanapuram to be with his mother. Some of his relatives were not pleased with Azariah marrying Anbu. The reason for their dissatisfaction was that traditions were not kept. For some of them it was a matter of ridicule that the marriage will be held without silk and silk garments, which is traditionally worn by men and women during Indian marriages. Both Azariah and his mother ignored such reactions from their relatives.

Anbu's fears did not leave her. After their betrothal, Azariah and Anbu corresponded with each other through letters. In one of her letters, she expressed her fear. In that letter she revealed her thoughts on the duties of married life, her responsibilities, joys and sorrows, and the burden in heart arising out of her thought as to how Azariah would treat her. Azariah wrote back to her briefly. Nevertheless, his brief reply is able to grant any young heart struggling with such doubts immediate assurance, truth, comfort known from experience, and peace. His brief reply was: "First, remember the Lord; then you remember me. Then you will receive peace." He used to share with her in his letters new ideas that came to his mind when he meditated on certain scripture passages. By writing such things, Anbu got to know the extent of her future husband's spiritual growth. This way, she was able to understand to some extent his excellent character.[8]

Azariah shared with her a beautiful idea on fixing the date of their marriage. The future apostle of Dornakal chose the date of his marriage as June 29 because the Church observed it as St. Peter's Day. The reason: the gospels reveal only Apostle Peter as the married apostle. We can only surmise that Azariah chose that date in the expectation that his wife Anbu would extend her full cooperation in his ministry as Peter's wife did in Peter's ministry.

As Azariah's brother Rev. Ambrose Thomas, head of the Meignanapuram CMS High School, had printed and pubished in Azariah's wedding invitation, the wedding of Azariah with Anbu was happily solemnized at 5:00 p.m. on June 29, 1898 at the CMS Church in Tirunelveli.[9]

The newly wedded couple hired a house in Palayamkottai and started their married life. God blessed them abundantly. As husband and wife, they were united in their hearts too. The married life they began that day continued joyfully by the abiding presence of Lord Jesus, Whom they both served and loved with all their hearts. It bore witness to Lord Jesus.

8. Letter dated April 20, 1898 to Mrs. Azariah.

9. Azariah's wedding invitation card preserved by Mrs. Azariah.

Several days after their wedding, Azariah had to travel. In the beginning, it was hard for both of them to be separated by Azariah's frequent travels. Their letters during those days depict the mental agony they suffered because of their separation. The letters clearly show how they loved Lord Jesus, and, for the Lord's sake, got accustomed to bearing that pain. "If it was God's will that they should be separated, then to be distressed by separation is an unacceptable sin unto God", they thought in course of time. To think like this, they must have become so mature in obeying God even in the beginning of their married life!

Azaraiah's letters of those days show how concerned he was about the growth of the spiritual life of his wife. Those letters also show how he cared that his wife's knowledge in worldly matters ought to grow. In his letters, he gave a summary of the blessed messages and sermons he heard during his travels, and his opinions. He praised the good characteristics of the great men he met. He retold the testimonies that he had witnessed, explained the customs of various communities who lived there, and gave her some new information.

Here we will show some of the things that he had described about the men he got acquainted with during his travels. "It was a great blessing just to sit close to Meyer," he wrote when he met F. B. Meyer, the Dean (chief pastor) of London's Westminster Abbey, who was conducting meetings in Chennai. "He doesn't talk much. He would ask some question; otherwise, he kept silent. His wife was a contrast to him".[10]

"Ah, what a sight to behold," he wrote about the famous Pandit Ramabai of Pune city. "She was short and small in her structure. Nevertheless, she managed 1,800 girls in her Home. Twelve European missionary women worked under her. All of them executed her commands. Her clothes were simple, her

10. Letter dated February 13, 1899.

bed a hard wooden plank! I thank the Lord who granted such a woman to India."[11]

"Pandit Chatterjee arrived here at a time when there was not one Christian in the entire district," he wrote about Pandit Chatterjee of Hoshiarpur. "He came here 38 years ago to serve the Lord. Today, there are 1,500 Christians here. Two indigenous pastors, a Girls Boarding School, a medical clinic for women, and an orphanage, - all operate under the supervision of Pandit Chatterjee. These institutions are fulfilling a magnificent ministry. There is not one European missionary here."[12]

We have mentioned a few samples of their work. If we were to write all the things done here, this book cannot contain them.

"His involvement in and enthusiasm for missionary work was greater than his involvement in other work. He had committed himself totally to it. He also received special gift for it."[13] It was his enthusiasm for missionary work that drew him to Student Voluntary Movement for Foreign Missions. Somehow the world must come to know Christ. The world must become His. Apart from doing whatever he could do to achieve this, he wanted to motivate others to work towards this end. The erstwhile YMCA was also influenced by the above-mentioned missionary movement. Therefore, it considered soul-winning as its primary duty. Through his job at the YMCA, Azariah made good use of the opportunities that he got to fulfill this duty. Yet, he was not satisfied. Even after about 200 years, Indian Christianity was still under the supervision of missionaries, and nourished and led by them. When was it going to pay back what it owed to the gospel? Azariah began to worry about this. He engaged himself in earnest prayer and supplications.

11. Letter dated September 18, 1906.
12. Letter dated August 22, 1906.
13. Eddy - Op. cit.

History tells us that once he visited Meignanapuram, where he had grown up. Here he walked on the coastal sand dunes through the dense palm grove. Kneeling down on the sand, he cried loudly in prayer with tears saying, “Lord, save India. Raise laborers, and guide us to minister.” Thus he prayed for long hours. Did he pray only once? Were his knees chafed only on the Meignanapuram sand dunes? Nay! He prayed wherever he went. He prayed at all times. Prayer was his breath. “His pining came forth in deep sighs.”

Days rolled on. Times passed by. On the one hand, he stood under the pressure of ‘the burden of missions’; on the other hand, he continually attended to his duties in his YMCA job, travelling all over. He kept praying for the Lord’s leading too.

Among the CMS missionaries in Tirunelveli, Rev. E. A. Douglas was a good friend of Azariah. He knew the burden in Azariah’s heart. He wished to somehow get Azariah engaged in CMS work and get him qualified to become a pastor. On 18th July 1901, he invited Azariah and spoke to him about it. Azariah left, saying that he would pray about it and answer him after some days.

Like Douglas, Rev. T. Walker also thought on the same lines to invite Azariah to pastoral ministry. At that time, he lived in Dohnavur training some students in pastoral ministry.

At the same time as Douglas and Azariah in Palayamkottai were engaged in a discussion on pastoral ministry, Walker in Dohnavur was writing a letter to Douglas. Next day, he dispatched that letter to Douglas. Douglas was immersed in wonder after he read the letter. At once, he sat down and penned this letterto Azariah:

> “It is surprising that this morning I received a letter from Rev. Walker on the same subject that we had

discussed last evening! In the letter he has expressed his confidence that you and J. Gnanayudham would enter pastoral ministry after studying the lessons required to become Assistant pastor. Therefore, now I officially invite you to give your consent to become a student of pastoral studies. In case you are coming, I strongly affirm that your pastoral ministry will be certainly welcome. If you confirm this, Walker, Rev. Carr and I would offer opportunities that can use all your abilities widely. Then, we believe, you would have accepted a permanent position. All things seem to indicate that you are being guided toward this. As soon as possible, send us your clear and firm reply. If you do so, then you can join Gnanayudham for the pastoral studies. If not, know that starting another class for pastoral studies may take a long time. If you reply at once, you will not be required to wait until the convening of the next administrative committee.

Yours

E. A. Douglas

19-7-'01"

Immediately, Azariah wrote to Eddy asking him if YMCA would relieve him. We don't know what Eddy replied for we don't have his reply letter. From another letter from Azariah it is evident that Eddy felt Azariah wished to keep his job at the YMCA. According to Eddy, Azariah thought that he was still not clear about God's will for him to enter pastoral ministry. So, Azariah continued to serve in the YMCA.

Meanwhile, Azariah continued to visit many places on official business, but he used these opportunities to conduct revival meetings. One day in 1902, he accepted an invitation from his friend Eddy to visit Yazhpanam (Jaffna). Since the beginning of the previous century, the American Mission there had been carrying on mission work. Consequently, they had established several institutions there, one of which was 'the Jaffna College'. Eddy and Azariah ministered among the students at the College. There was an excellent YMCA branch at the college. With the efforts of the student members of that YMCA branch, the local city Church and the student community had met together as a Council. Then they had started a Missionary Society to minister in foreign lands. The mission field they chose to work in was Thondi, a village in Madurai district of Tamilnadu state in India. Indigenous missionaries from Jaffna evangelized Thondi and planted churches there. When he came to know about this, Azariah rejoiced and praised the Lord. As he was praising the Lord, he thought about something and kept thinking.

His heart cried.

CHAPTER 3

AZARIAH, THE PROPHET

"Here I am; send me" Isaiah 6: 8

"When we study the Acts of the Apostles intently, the truth becomes evident that our Lord Jesus Christ established the Church only to proclaim the gospel. If the Church lacks interest in it, whatever other deeds it may do, these would be futile; and it is in a dead state. On the contrary, if we bring people into the Church by proclaiming the gospel, then we will have life. That vibrant life will empower us to accomplish all the good works that, we as a church, desire to do. Alas! Now we are not able to do anything. And what we do, we are unable to effectively fulfill. If we look for the reason, we will know that the root is being eaten away. What is the evil that is eating away the root? Our Church that was established in the world only to propagate the gospel is not fulfilling its fundamental duty. Let us make our congregations witnesses to the gospel. It does not matter if they do not know how to preach. Let them come and stand in the place where the gospel is preached. That would amount to witnessing."[1]

"The church that does not proclaim the gospel to others is a useless, dead church." This was Azariah's firm belief. Little Jaffna town has a foreign mission. And that mission serves in our country. On the one hand, we are negligent; on the other hand, Jaffna is teaching us by doing what we ought to have

1. A few words extracted from Azariah's sermon to ministers in the Nashik Diocese.

done. The Tirunelveli Church with about 100,000 Christians and a history of 130 years boasts of its beautiful church buildings, towers, educational institutions for boys and girls, colleges, schools for the deaf-and-dumb, schools for the blind, and hospitals. It boasts of city churches and village churches. It boasts of multitudes of pastors, catechists, Bible women and various other workers. Jaffna is too small to be compared to the Tirunelveli church in terms of its structure and age. Yet, Jaffna church is vibrant and lively. Is my own church dead?..."

A flood of thoughts ran through Azariah's mind. He wept. Tears rolled down and sank into the sands of the Jaffna seashore. His tears dissolved in the waves knocking his knees. God heard the prayers of Azariah as he knelt and prayed with tears. Having heard his prayers, God demanded Azariah's heart. Azariah promptly gave his heart to God. Then and there, before the outstretched arms of God, Azariah surrendered his life to mission work. After returning to his country, Azariah kept thinking on these matters.

Has the Tirunelveli church never done missionary work? Why? Of course, it did! And it did many times. Did Azariah know about these? We have no idea. During the time of Rev. Rhenius, he sent a catechist to Cochin. During this time (1834-1839), the catechist started a small church there. Later, this church blossomed into a large church following the work of Rev. Henry Harley (1839-1871).[2] About 20 years later, in 1852, some catechists who ministered in the areas of Surandai and Pavur, on their own evangelized a certain hill tribe called *Travancore Malayarasar*. Motivated by missionaries in Surandai and Nalloor, these catechists brought hundreds of *Malayarasar* tribe people into the church. Finally, in the 1860s, people of the tribe were committed to the C. M. S. missionaries in Kottayam. In 1834, Rev. Rhenius sent some catechists to assist the ministers of the American Mission in Madurai. It was the Tirunelveli church that commissioned its

2. CMS mission in Cochin.

pastors and catechists to the Madurai mission for the next 20 years and helped in the growth of the Madurai church. The Tirunelveli church sent funds as well as many catechists and several pastors to 'Ceylon Coolie Mission', 'the Mauritius Mission', 'the Koya Mission in Andhra' and other missions, and thus took part in the work of these missions.

We have no idea whether Azariah knew or knew not this history of the Tirunelveli church. As an aggressive Indian Christian, Azariah was not at all satisfied with the contribution of the Tirunelveli church to mission work. These were the times when Tirunelveli church could accomplish nothing without the impetus provided by the missionaries. Without the favor, generosity, permission and support of Westerners, Nellai Christians could do nothing on their own. They were not even trained to do things on their own. There was no lack of celebrated church leaders in Tirunelveli. It is true that renowned luminaries among pastors appeared now and then. Nevertheless, they could accomplish nothing independent of the missionaries. Until Azariah appeared on the scene, Nellai Christians could accomplish nothing great on their own.

Please do not lightly imagine that Azariah conceived something in his mind, gathered some people, and started the Indian Missionary Society. He carried a heavy burden and suffered the travails of child birth before he started the Society. He spent nights of tears and cries in prayer as he knelt between the dwarf palm trees of Meignanapuram and on the sandy beaches of Jaffna. "Lord, I have surrendered my life to you. Now what am I to do? Please reveal your will to me," he said as he waited upon the Lord seeking an answer to his prayer. What tears! What lament! He had no dreams of setting up the Indian Missionary Society. One thing he knew: God was calling him to do something. But, what was he to do? He did not know. Why has God not revealed it? "There is some shortcoming in me" he said to himself. "But what is that shortcoming? I am unable to find it. Reveal it, O God."

Ah! Those were the days that a great unknown burden was pressing on his heart. His heart melted in tears.

"Whyareyoucastdown,Omysoul,andwhyareyouinturmoil within me," cried the Psalmist in Psalm 42:5. Azariah's gripe was similar to the Psalmist's cry.

With whom could he share his heart's desire except with his wife, whom he considered to be his 'life'? One of those days, he visited Kodaikanal with Eddy. The pressure of mission work lay heavily on his heart. He could not sleep. Waking up, he knelt down and prayed seeking God's guidance. "Lord, what do you want me to do?" he said in his prayer. "What is my shortcoming? Have I not been filled by the Spirit of God?" But he received no answer.

The following morning, he wrote a letter to his wife: "Ah, that I may be filled by the Holy Spirit! Ah, if only I would be devoid of my own fleshly thought, plan and words! My beloved, I am scared of my own self. It is true that I trust in the bright radiant fact that our old man has been crucified with our dear Lord. How I long to know it experientially in my daily life. Does this mean that I should hate myself daily? Here I find myself helpless. There is 'self' in every prayer, sermon, work, and in everything else, isn't it? Please pray for me, my beloved. Will you not pray with burden that God may teach me to wholly hate my own self?[3]

"Hope in God: for I shall again praise Him, my salvation and my God" wrote the Psalmist in Psalm 42: 5. Like the Psalmist, Azariah made this his determination. "He hoped in God." His wife Anbu also prayed for him in the same manner. The time was near for God to reveal His will.

Azariah had some valuable friends in Palayamkottai. He opened his heart to some of them and sought their prayer. They

3. Letter to his wife 1902.

not only prayed, but also often discussed among themselves as to how the Tirunelveli church could fulfill its duties. In the evenings, many of them who were members of the YMCA met in Osborne Memorial School. They shared various ideas among themselves. When the Tirunelveli church itself is supported by Western missionary societies, how can it start a society and run it? When the Tirunelveli Christians are not able to support their church and are dependent on foreign funds, will it be an attainable goal for them to do mission work, establish a church and support it? Many expressed such doubts.

Azariah had some firm convictions on this matter:

1. It is a wrong principle that a church should attempt to self-propagate only after it becomes fully self-reliant.

2. It is wrong to believe that a church that gets involved in mission work will lose its own income, the income that had made it self-reliant.

3. It is an undeniable fact that mission work will only strengthen a church's attempts to become self-reliant.[4]

His friends who agreed with these principles started gathering for prayer. They continued in prayer for weeks and months.

Let's quote from what Bishop Azariah himself wrote about the history of the Tirunelveli Indian Missionary Society:

"The thought that often arose in the mind of many God's children for 500 years was that if Tirunelveli Church has to be blessed in a special way, it has to obey the final commandment of our dear Lord. At that time, such a thought was not yet affirmed because of the doubt on whether the Tirunelveli Church was qualified to start such a work. All we can now say is it was not the Lord's appointed time. On the contrary,

4. 'Self-support in relation to Self-propagation' – a Pamphlet by Azariah in manuscript.

towards the end of 1902, such a thought rose again in the hearts of some God's children, who shared the thought with their fellow-believers. In one accord, they concluded that now was the time to start such a work. In wonder, the respondents revealed that they also had been considering this for some time. From then on, those sharing this thought began to pray about it daily. Thereafter, in order to conscientize the entire Tirunelveli Church about this responsibility, the February 1903 edition of Narpothagam published a short write-up under the title "Call to Serve in Foreign Mission". It explained in detail the importance of the gracious Lord's final commandment, and Tirunelveli Church's responsibility regarding this. While reconciling the objections against foreign mission work, it also narrated the blessings that can accrue to us when we carry out this work. This was also published as a booklet to be distributed among the local Circle Presidents and VIPs who were not subscribers to Narpothagam. The booklet also appealed to the sympathizers to contact the Editor.[5] The purpose of carrying out this exercise was to know how many persons from the district would support foreign mission work in case it started.

"Many from the district, who read these and whose hearts God had stirred up, became passionate about it. In February, many of them travelled to Palayamkottai to attend the Society Council meetings and other meetings. Those who considered that a Missionary Society should be started to meet the goal of this publication, and who prayed for it daily for several months, met for prayer for three days. In consultation with Rev. E. S. Carr, Rev. F. W. Freid, Rev. E. A. Douglas, and others, they also drew the aims and objectives as well as the bye-laws of the Society, and decided on these in an orderly fashion. Finally, all those who sympathized with this cause met in the evening of February 12 in a Y.M.C.A. room at Tirunelveli.[6] They discussed each and everyaim, objective and bye-law of the Society, which had been set in order. They decided on the

5. To the Editor, Narpothagam.

6. In those days the central room of Osborne Memorial School in Tirunelveli was used for Y.M.C.A. work in the evenings.

name Tirunelveli Indian Missionary Society, and established the Society in the Lord. They determined the main aims and objectives of the Society to be: (i) to stir up Tirunelveli Christians to exercise concern in the work of the propagation of the gospel; (ii) to send servants of God to places in India and abroad, which are not yet evangelized. Eight pastors and 20 lay members from 16 different places participated in that meeting. This was the humble beginning of the Society. The loving Father, Who does not despise even the humblest service done for His glory, accepted this ministry done in weakness. Without considering our worthiness or unworthiness, He poured out His abundant grace on it. The very thought of this makes us duty-bound to fall at His feet and praise Him in all humility."[7]

According to the above report, Tirunelveli Indian Missionary Society was established, neither in Palayamkottai C.M.S. Rest House nor in the Diocesan Press building, but prayerfully in a room in the Osborne School. Also, it was not established by just six persons, namely, Azariah, Anbudaiyan, Appasamy, Arthur, Asirvatham R. V.,[8]and Asirvatham M. It was started by 20 persons.

Lay members:

V. S. Azariah; J. Anbudaiyan; A. S. Appasamy;

G. J. Arthur; R. V. Asirvatham, J. M. Devadason;[9]

S. D. Perinbam (Donavur apothecary or pharmacist);

J. S. Devasahayam (Palayamkottai);

S. K. Deivasigamani;

---

7. A report written by the then Secretary of the Society Azariah, in the first Anniversary Report of the Indian Missionary Society, pages 9-11.
8. Later he became a Pastor.
9. The first Editor of the magazine Jeevathaneer (Living Waters), donated the printing paper needed to print Indian Missionary Society's magazine Suvisesha Prabala Varthamani. He died all of a sudden in 1904. His death was the first great loss for IMS.

Samuel Packianathan; [10]

P. Gnanamuthu (Ukkiramankottai);

V. Devasahayam (Parvathiyapuram);

J. S. Madhuram; V. Samuel (S. T. C.);

J. H. Patterpron*; V. J. Dyer*;

M. Gnanaprakasam (Nalloor);

D. Anbudaiyan; Appavu David;

D. Devadason (Suviseshapuram). *

Pastors: M. Asirvatham (Pannaivilai); S. M. Devadoss (Palayamkottai); A. S. Devapriyam (Ambasamudram); D. S. David (Nalloor); P. G. Simeon (Suviseshapuram); G. Manickam (Palayamkottai); S. G. Madhuram (Virudhupatti); J. Albert (Srivilliputhur).

Please note that throughout the report Azariah maintained a low profile, and did not project himself. Although he was the prime mover in starting the Indian Missionary Society, he gave prominence to others who prayed and took efforts.

Azariah was appointed as the Society's first Secretary, J. Anbudaiyan as the Treasurer, Tirunelveli Bishop as the Patron, Rev. E. S. Carr as the Vice-Patron, and A. S. Appasamy as President. Rev. Joseph David of Meignanapuram, Rev. P. G. Simeon of Suviseshapuram, Rev. D. S. David of Nalloor, and Rev. M. Asirvatham of Pannaivilai were appointed as Vice-Presidents. Rev. V. Gnanamuthu of Azhvaneri, Rev. A. S. Devapriyam of Ambasamudram, Rev. J. Albert, Rev. S. G. Madhuram, Rev. S. M. Devadoss, Mr. J. S. Devasahayam, Mr. S. D. Perinbam, Mr. G. J. Arthur, and Mr. M. Gnanaprakasam of Nalloor were appointed as Committee members.

10. Later, they became trained Pastors.*

Those appointed as **local secretaries** were:

Nalloor circle	: M. Gnanaprakasam, Preacher & Investigator.
Surandai circle	: J. V. Devavaram, Preacher
Suviseshapuram	: D. Devadason, Writer.
Pannaivilai	: Rev. M. Asirvatham.
Meignanapuram	: A. Masilamani, Preacher
Tirunelveli City	: Moses Sreenivasagam.
Tirunelveli C. M. College	: Macaulay Thomas.

Local Secretaries (Women)

Palayamkottai	: Mrs. G. Manickam Ammal.
	: Mrs. Martin Luther Ammal.
Suviseshapuram	: Mrs. P. G. Simeon Ammal.
Nalloor	: Mrs. D. S. David Ammal.
Surandai	: Mrs. D. M. Packianathan Ammal.
Meignanapuram	: Mrs. Vedhanayagam Ammal.
Pannaivilai	: Mrs. M. Asirvatham Ammal.

Among them, Moses Sreenivasagam was the brother of Azariah's wife. Macaulay Thomas was the son of Azariah's brother. Mrs. Vedhanayagam Ammal was Azariah's mother.

The first Life Member was Mr. A. S. Appasamy. Next to him, in 1903, J. Anbudaiyan became the second Life Member. In 1904, S. D. Perinbam became the third Life Member. In 1906, M. Devasahayam of Kailasapuram became the fourth Life Member.

The Constitution of the Society that was agreed upon on the first day.[11]

11. Tirunelveli Indian Missionary Society report 1903, pages 3-6.

The Bye-laws of Tirunelveli Indian Missionary Society

Name:

This Society shall be called **Tirunelveli Indian Missionary Society.**

Aims and Objectives:

This indigenous effort aims at developing in the indigenous church a passion to propagate the gospel in India and abroad.

Members:

(i) All indigenous, communicant members of the Tirunelveli Church can become members of the Society.

(ii) Among the above-mentioned persons, a resident of Tirunelveli for a year, who has paid his or her annual subscription to the Church, will be considered as a member for that year only. Such persons have the right to issue their consent letter.

Honorary Members:

All other Christians who subscribe to the aims and objectives of the Society and pay their annual subscription to the Church will be considered as Honorary Members.

Life Members:

A member who pays Rs.100 (Rupees One Hundred) at a time will be considered as a Life Member.

Staff:

- A Patron, a Vice-Patron, a President, Vice-Presidents, a Secretary and a Treasurer, along with the annually elected Committee, will administer the Society.

• If the Bishop of Tirunelveli – Madurai, having already been Honorary Member of the Society, consents to be the Patron of the Society, he shall be the Patron of the Society.

• If any president of the C. M. S. district councils, having already been Honorary Member of the Society, consents to be the Vice-President, he or she shall be the Vice-President of the Society.

• An indigenous Christian elected by the Annual General Body meeting annually shall be the President of the Society.

• The Annual General Body meeting shall elect four Vice-Presidents from among the Members of the Society who are already Circle Presidents.

• The Committee shall nominate the Secretary and the Treasurer on an annual basis. The Committee shall nominate the Secretary and the Treasury from within the Committee or outside.

Committee

• The President, the Vice-Presidents, the Secretary, the Treasurer and ten other members shall constitute the Committee.

• The Patron and the Vice-Patron shall be members of the Committee by virtue of their offices.

• In times of emergency, the Committee may nominate a Secretary or a Treasurer to raise funds. A person so nominated shall be deemed to be a member of the Committee.

• If there is a staff vacancy or a vacancy in the Committee, the Committee is authorized to fill the vacancy until the next Annual General Body meeting takes place.

Duties:

• In the absence of the President, one of the Vice-Presidents shall preside over all Committee meetings.

• It shall be the responsibility of the Secretary to record the Minutes of the Committee meetings. He or she shall also be responsible for all correspondence and communication relating to Committee matters. In general, the Secretary shall operate the affairs of the Society under the orders of the Committee.

• It is the responsibility of the Treasurer to keep the assets and accounts of the Society, and to disburse the money approved in writing by the signatories, that is, the President and the Secretary, with the permission of the Committee.

Annual General Body meeting:

The General Body of the Society shall meet annually on the second Wednesday of July. The Secretary shall, at this time, read the Report of the Previous Year's activities. The Treasurer shall submit the Annual accounts of the Society. The President, the Vice-Presidents, and the Committee shall be elected at this time.

Committee meetings:

The Committee shall meet at least once in three months in a year.

The President and the Secretary shall jointly convene the Committee for any day.

The head of the Committee has the right to cast a second vote in the event of a tie.

Election:

• Election shall always be based on the votes cast.

• The Committee that is winding up that year shall nominate three members of the Society as the ad-hoc Nomination Committee. To be elected as the President, he or she should receive not more than two nominations. The ad-hoc Nomination Committee shall nominate not more than 15 members to be elected as Committee members. If the Annual General Body agrees, members can add other nominations. The same staff and Committee members can be re-elected.

Auditing of Accounts:

The accounts of the Society shall be audited annually by two persons appointed by the Committee.

Missionaries

The Secretarial Committee should be informed about matters relating to persons who consecrate their lives for missionary service. It is the Committee that determines the acceptance of those who consecrate themselves for missionary service, as well as their training, their postings, and their salaries.

The Doctrine of the Society:

The Society shall completely follow the doctrine of the pure gospel.

Amendments to the Bye-laws of the Society:

No bye-law of the Society shall be amended without the unanimous consent of the Committee or the consent of three-fourth members of the Annual General Body meeting. The amendments passed by the Committee must be ratified by the remaining members of the Annual General Body meeting immediately thereafter.

It was Azariah who drafted the Bye-laws. He, along with Appasamy and Anbudaiyan, showed the draft to Rev. Carr, Rev. Freid and Rev. Douglas. Following their advice, they made a few changes. Finally, the Annual General Body meeting held in July that year ratified the Bye-laws of the Society.

The Indian Missionary Society's Annual Reports published during 1904 to 1909, reveals the magnificence of the matchless work completed by Azariah as its Secretary.

The news of the birth of the Tirunelveli Indian Missionary Society spread like wild fire in the Nellai Church. People were filled with joy. Many C.M.S. pastors, catechists and other ministers vowed to pray all their lifetime for the Society and to support it financially. Most of them kept their vows until the end of their lives. It is a known fact that more than anything else, their prayers were the reason for its today's growth and for the full blessing of these efforts.

Having established the Society, they now had to determine the territory of ministry. Azariah kept it in his prayers. He visited Coimbatore and Salem (including Dharmapuri) districts in search of potential mission fields. Then he visited places outside his home state of Tamilnadu. Finally he concluded that Manukot Taluk (sub-division) known as Mahboobabad was the ideal mission field. It was located in the Southeast of the kingdom of the erstwhile Nawab (king) of Hyderabad, which now forms a large part of the state of Telangana; the Taluk (sub-division) was a large forest area. Most of its inhabitants were uneducated. A vast majority of the people lived in villages and served the local landlords. The backward people in the villages were extremely poor. They were uncivilized.

Azariah envisaged Manukot town as the center of the mission. It was seen as a large village (or as a small town) in those parts. There was a railway station there.

Later, when early missionaries were sent there, the local Muslims opposed the coming of missionaries to their village. So, this move of making Manukot as the center of the mission was given up. Dornakal town was chosen as the center of mission work.

In those days, Andhra, as it was known at that time, (including the kingdom of Nizam), Karnataka, North Kerala, and Tamilnadu (with the exception of the districts of Ramanathapuram, Tirunelveli and Kanyakumari) were all in the Diocese of the Bishop in Chennai. Beingpart of that Diocese, Tirunelveli Christians, who were a part of the Anglican Church, had to obtain prior permission and blessing from the

Bishop in Chennai. Therefore, Azariah visited Chennai to meet with Bishop Whitehead. That was the beginning of yet another friendship, which, humanly speaking, paved the way for Azariah's future elevation. Whitehead, who witnessed Azariah's enthusiasm and his love for his Lord, gladly granted the permission that Azariah sought. He also opened his Diocese to the Society's missionaries.

Azariah now needed missionaries to start the Society's work. The Secretary of the Society, its Council, and many Nellai Christians prayed that the Lord Himself will choose and send forth the first servant of God. One of those who prayed in this manner was a school-teacher called Samuel Packianathan. He was an excellent saint. He was one of the early pioneers of the Children's Society. He was also the Secretary of that Society at that time.

The Lord spoke to Samuel Packianathan, and he dedicated himself to the Lord saying, "Lord, send me". Knowing Packianathan's devotion, enthusiasm and thirst for souls, Azariah was thrilled. The Children's Society was not willing to relieve Packianathan. However, they rejoiced that they were blessed indeed to provide the first missionary of their Missionary Society. So, they bid him farewell.

On March 9, 1904, Samuel Packianathan was commissioned as the first missionary of the Indian Missionary Society and consecrated to the Lord at a Special Commissioning Service at Palayamkottai's Holy Trinity Church. A month later, on April 12 he arrived at Khammamedu near Dornakal. He learned Telugu language. Within two months he set his abode in Dornakal's Old Liquor Warehouse. From there he propagated the gospel.

In1904, Azariah started a monthly magazine titled Gospel Propagation Gazette. Its purpose was to inform Nellai Church members and others all the above-mentioned news. Thus he spread news about the Indian Missionary Society, and helped increase the number of its supporters.The Society grew.

In the following two years, two more missionaries were sent: (i) D. Devasahayam on April 5, 1905, and (ii) Solomon Packianathan on August 11, 1906. Solomon Packianathan was the younger brother of Samuel Packianathan. Devashayam dedicated himself to missionary service having received direct invitation from Azariah.

Samuel Packianathan's ministry bore fruit within a year. On June 26, 1905, forty souls from seven families were welcomed as children of Christ in Parole village, and were ready to be baptized. On August 6, 1906, fifteen men and eighteen women were added to the Church after being baptized by Bishop Whitehead. They were the first-fruits of the Indian Missionary Society. Moreover, many from Meduthapalle, Savattapalle and Dottalakoodam joined the church and were prepared for baptism. In 1906, 302 persons from ten villages were prepared to witness in the waters of baptism. In 1907, there were eleven villages having Christians; in 1908, there were 20 villages; in 1909, there were 28 villages with a Christian population.

In 1906, Azariah started a movement called "Workers Fellowship". Its aim was to pray regularly, raise funds and muster support in Palayamkottai. This movement began to grow as a society comprising both men and women. They met together every Thursday in the church, and prayed for hours.

From 1907, members of the society conducted the festival of Indian Missionary Society's Annual Sales. It is common knowledge that it continues to be celebrated without fail every year since then. Moreover, members of this society visited many churches in Tirunelveli, spoke about the missionary society, and mobilized support for the society.

Many Tirunelveli C. M. S. missionaries were not concerned about Indian Missionary Society in the latter's early days. In the Annual Report of 1903 submitted by the missionaries Camper, Ardill, Carr, Walker, Shafter and Keyworth, none of them mentioned about the formation of the Society. Perhaps they thought in derision, "Can a few Indians start something together? And will it flourish?"

On July 9, 1903, when Tirunelveli Christians gathered for the 'Mango Society' festival, Mr. A.S. Appasamy spoke in the first meeting of the Indian Missionary Society: "We are all very glad that the Tirunelveli Church has given birth to a baby after many years." After this, Bishop Morley[12] said: "I was afraid that the Lord may extinguish the lamp of the Tirunelveli Church if she did not become a missionary church. Today, that fear has fled from me.

The strength of this Society is that it has been formed as an Indian Society by some enthusiastic eminent people of the Tirunelveli Church." His speech gave the seal of approval of

12. This was his last sermon delivered in Tirunelveli.

the Church. This gave Azariah great joy.

None of the missionaries, except Rev. Douglas, referred to this joyful occasion in their reports to the C. M. S. Society.

In the first five months people had donated Rs.1,000 to Azariah for the Society. Out of this, only Rs. 70 was the contribution of Europeans.[13]

If this was the position of the C.M.S. missionaries, what would have been the position of the S.P.G. missionaries? It took three years for the latter to evince interest in the Indian Missionary Society. After three years, in 1906, Nazareth district[14] showed the way. "It is our duty to support the Indian Missionary Society started entirely by Indians," said an eminent missionary Rev. Arthur Margoschis emphatically. He urged his diocesan people to support the Society. The following year, the diocese of Tuticorin and Idaiyankudy extended their support to the Society. In 1908, Sawyerpuram, Christianpet, Mudalur, Pudukottai and Pudhiyamputhur diocesan areas lent their support. On March 25, 1909, the Tirunelveli S.P.G. Council that met in Nazareth under the leadership of the new missionary Rev. Carlin Wilfred Weston passed a resolution, saying, "Along with the C.M.S. churches, S.P.G. churches should also support I.M.S." This truly qualified its name Tirunelveli Indian Missionary Society.[15]

Although Azariah assumed the position of Secretary of the Indian Missionary Society, he did not give up his job at the YMCA. Though he wanted to quit his YMCA job, Eddy did not consent. Therefore, he continued with his official travels.

In 1903, Azariah was appointed as the Joint Secretary of the All India YMCA National Council. Consequently, he had to travel across India. He visited Sri Lanka. Wherever he went, his cry was, "Rise and shine!" However, when he

13. Report of E. A. Douglas, 1903.

14. Now known as Circle.

15. SPG Provincial Council report, 1909.

realized that there were no takers for this, he recorded these incidents regretfully. North Indian church leaders, in particular, disappointed him. In 1905 he traveled to Delhi, Agra, Tundla and other places in North India, addressing churches there, and stressing the need for evangelistic ministry. “What you say is not possible in Indian churches,” said a Baptist church pastor in Tundla (Uttar Pradesh) after the service. That pastor held a Master of Arts degree.

“There is the need to make people progress,” he said. “First of all, we need to uplift them in many ways. After that, we may expect Evangelistic ministry.” The C.M.S. pastor in Aligarh spoke in like manner. Nevertheless, Azariah did not lose heart. He continued conducting Revival meetings and Inspirational meetings motivating people to do the work of an Evangelist. He held such meetings in several places across India.

On August 15, 1905, he addressed a large gathering at the Forman Christian College auditorium in Lahore (now in Pakistan). “It is highly necessary that Indian Christians reach out to Indians,” said Azariah in an inspirational talk. “It is not the prerogative of Westerners to proclaim Christ around the world; it is the duty of Indians too. It is my expectation that a National Missionary Society will be formed to fulfill this responsibility.”[16]

It was Eddy’s plan to form a National Missionary Society. Both the friends contemplated on this matter, and prayed about it.

Both of them propagated the matter during their travels. “Those who consent to this are welcome to attend a joint-consultation meet at William Carey’s renowned College in Serampore, Bengal (now West Bengal),” they announced. Particularly, from October, they began to inform people in many places about it. Accordingly, an invitation signed by

16. G. V. Job in ‘Samuel Vedhanayagam Azariah’, Page 20.

eminent Indian Christians Professor Samuel Sathyanathan, Kallicharan Banerjee and Raja Maharajsingh was sent out to several leaders. On Christmas day December 25, 1905, sixteen persons from various places met at Serampore College. A few came from Burma (now Myanmar) and Sri Lanka too. First Azariah spoke about the need to form National Missionary Society. "If it has to be an Indian Society, it should be supported with Indian money, it should be headed by an Indian, and the gospel must be proclaimed in an Indian manner," said Azariah underlining the three fundamental principles. After discussing the matter for a little while, they prayed intensely. "In the name of the Lord, let us form the National Missionary Society based on these three principles," proposed Sirajudeen from Lahore. Two other leaders K. T. Paul and J. Chitambar seconded the proposal. The general body unanimously endorsed the proposal. National Missionary Society took shape that very moment, and Azariah was nominated as its General Secretary.

Having wholeheartedly accepted this responsibility, Azariah began to travel to different parts of India proclaiming the Society's missionary news. He also mobilized support for it across the nation. Later, he co-opted his friend K. T. Paul as its Joint Secretary, and worked along with him. He started missionary work in the Punjab, United Province (today's Maharashtra) and Bombay Rajdhani (today's Uttar Pradesh) and caused the ministry to flourish there. He also attempted to start the ministry in Salem and Hyderabad.[17]

Thus, he served as unpaid Secretary of both the Indian Missionary Society and the National Missionary Society after instituting them. He also continued to be the Joint Secretary of the YMCA Society. At a YMCA conference, he met a student called John Williams. Being aware of John's godliness and conduct, Azariah appointed him as the missionary in Montgomery in the Punjab (now Sahiwal in the Punjab, Pakistan). John Williams was the first missionary of the

17. Eddy – op. cit..

National Missionary Society.

Azariah did not slacken his involvement in the World Student Christian Movement (SCM). In April 1907, he visited Tokyo at the invitation of the scholar John Raleigh Mott to attend their conference. Azariah attended the conference; there, his distinctions were clear for people to see. At the end of the conference, he was appointed as the vice-president of the International Christian Student Movement. From then on, Azariah began to find a place in the history of the global Church.

Despite assuming various responsibilities in this manner, there was no shortcoming in his service to any one of them. He kept travelling on account of his involvement in the Indian Missionary Society, YMCA, and the National Missionary Society. He continued mobilizing moral support and monetary support for the missionary societies, and also kept looking for new missionaries. At the same time, he kept visiting the YMCA branches, always encouraging them, always opening new YMCA branches, and conducting Revival meetings.

CHAPTER 4

AZARIAH, THE PRIEST

““Let your priests be clothed with righteousness…and your saints shout for joy” Psalm 132: 9

At one time, Azariah and Samuel Paramanandam conducted meetings in Coimbatore callling upon people to dedicate themselves to missionary service. Later, Azariah spoke in a similar meeting in Chennai. “I call upon others to dedicate themselves to missionary service,” thought Azariah. “But why should I not go for missionary service?” He was certain that God was calling him again. At once, he decided, in the Lord, to go to Dornakal as a missionary.

At once, he began to take action on his decision. He informed his dear wife and his close friend Anbudaiyan about his decision. His wife Anbu was worried about the education of her growing children. Yet, considering her husband’s enthusiasm for evangelistic ministry and her own enthusiasm for it, which was no less than her husband’s, she gave her wholehearted consent to his idea. Anbudaiyan felt sad that if Azariah left for Dornakal, it would not be easy to find a suitable person to act as Secretary in his place. In those days, he often visited Azariah and expressed his worry. They argued about it, but always they closed with prayer.

Azariah disclosed his decision in the administrative meeting of the Indian Missionary Society. He requested them to accept him as a missionary and send him to Dornakal.

Several members of the Society expressed their worries much as Anbudaiyan had done. Yet, in general, they welcomed his decision. Azariah's heart was filled with joy.

That day, Azariah and Anbu felt that the Lord was sending them to his work just as the Lord had sent Paul and Barnabas to his ministry, and they praised God from the depth of their hearts.

If he was going to Dornakal as missionary, he needed to give up his job at NMS and YMCA. Members of both the societies were sad. Though Eddy was sad that Azariah was leaving them, he recalled Azariah's thirteen years of service to YMCA, praised God and bid farewell to Azariah. "YMCA is more indebted to Azariah than Azariah is indebted to YMCA," wrote Eddy. "YMCA's aim is to train people to handle responsible jobs. YMCA opened many opportunities for Azariah to address meetings in colleges, cities, our branches, and in churches. YMCA trained him and gave him a wide field of service to minister to God. We praise God for Azariah, and pray to God that he may be filled with divine blessings in his new job."[1]

Supporters of the National Missionary Society felt sad that Azariah would be confining himself to a small place as missionary to Dornakal. "If he continues to serve YMCA or NMS, he will get opportunities to serve on a larger scale across India," they said. "He is losing those opportunities." Others thought, "Why not merge NMS and IMS?" "It is not possible for members of various churches to take care of the gospel ministry done on behalf of one single church, and that through a common institution," Azariah said. "Every section of the Church can get involved wholeheartedly in the work of the gospel only when it is done on behalf of that section of the Church. There will be a sense of ownership. Moreover, it is good that every church invites its own members to get

1. Eddy – Op. Cit..

involved in its own gospel work." Anyhow, members of the NMS Society also were united in their hearts to bid farewell to Azariah with their blessings. After this, Azariah met the Bishop in Chennai and informed him of his decision, and received his blessings.

Meanwhile, the Dornakal ministry had not only grown, but also had expnanded. Sreenivasan and Devathanjam were two young Brahmin men from Tirunelveli, who had recently become Christians. On July 26, 1907, they were sent as missionaries to Dornakal along with Samuel Packianathan, who had come to Tirunelveli, and was returning to Dornakal. About 18 months later, in January 1909, C. K. Muthusamy followed them to Dornakal after he had successfully completed his training at the Nazareth Craftsmanship factory. His job was to train new Christians in carpentry so that they may eke out their livelihood as Carpenters.

Isaiah and his wife Prema, both of whom were 'mission children' trained at the Dornakal Teachers School were appointed as Catechists in Pirol. Isaac and his wife Mariamma, who were similarly trained, were sent to Silveru as Catechists. In its fifth year, the Missionary Society started Pazhayar Mission ministry. The Bishop in Chennai Whitehead thought highly of Azariah as 'a great man' because Azariah gave up his comforts, glory, and opportunities for advancement in order to serve as a missionary in Dornakal, where he had very little comforts, where his glory would fade away, and where he would have no career advancements. The Bishop thought that he had found the right man for the position that he had envisaged in his mind. But he did not reveal his thought to Azariah on that day.

Whitehead decided to ordain Azariah as Assistant Pastor before the latter became a missionary in Dornakal. Azariah also thought that this should be the will of God, and consented to this. It was also decided that Azariah should be paid a salary equal to what the YMCA was paying him, and that IMS and the Bishop in Chennai should contribute to his salary. In preparation for his ordination as Assistant Pastor, Azariah was successfully trained by Whitehead when the latter spent his summer in Ootacamund in the Nilgiris district. On June 29, 1909, the day of his wedding anniversary, Azariah was ordained as an Assistant Pastor. The previous night, Whitehead revealed that he had in his heart plans for Azariah's future ministry. When Azariah heard this, his heart began to palpitate. He could not sleep. He was confused with fear in his mind, bewilderment, astonishment, hesitation and anxiety about his suitability for the task. Kneeling down at home, he communed with his God for a long time. "Lord may your will be done," he said, committing himself to God. And he went to sleep.

After receiving his ordination as Assistant Pastor, he returned to Palayamkottai. As usual he continued to be engaged in his routine jobs. He did not reveal to his dear wife what he had heard from Bishop Whitehead. Nor did he reveal it to his dear friend Anbudaiyan.

At six in the evening on July 15, 1909, the Annual General Body meeting of the IMS was held in Palayamkottai CMS Centenary Hall. It was presided over by the Bishop in Tirunelveli-Madurai. It began with a gospel song. Muthuvel from Colombo read Psalm 67 from the Bible. Idayankulam Circle Pastor Rev. D. M. Packianathan prayed. After the Presidential speech by its President Mr. A. S. Appasamy, Panneerkulam Rev. A. Savarimuthu read a report on the affairs of the IMS Executive Board. After this, they sang a hymn. Then, IMS missionary Mr. Solomon Packianathan, who had come on furlough, spoke about the work of the Dornakal School. The special speaker for the evening, Pasumalai pastor F. Kingsbury delivered a challenging sermon based on Revelation 21: 2.

As Azariah stood facing the audience, Rev. P. G. Simeon,

B.A. read the Counsel given by the Society's Executive Board to him who was leaving to assume charge as Dornakal missionary. It was a soul-stirring reading for all. In his farewell speech, Rev. Azariah shared how he and his wife were glad to go to Dornakal on the assurance that the Lord had called them to the Telugu territory. As he was going there as a representative of the Tirunelveli Church, he was confident to be strengthened by the prayers of many Tirunelveli Christians. He fully trusted that both young and old as well as pastors would visit Dornakal. The Right Reverend Bishop said that they were delighted to see the work of the Society grow. Rev. Camper prayed committing Rev. Azariah to God's protection and divine guidance, and for the furtherance of the work of the Society. They sang the song, "Climb the Himalayan Mountain" when the Offertory was taken. The offerings amounted to Rs.65-11-8½ (Rupee – Anna – Paisa). The meeting was dissolved after Benediction by the Bishop.[2]

From the 16th of that month, Rev. Azariah started preparing to leave for Dornakal. It was decided that at the outset his wife and children would not accompany him to Dornakal, but they would move there after Azariah made arrangements for his family's stay. He made arrangements to take with him a man called Suviseshamuthu to assist him at the new place. His family and friends saw him off at the Tirunelveli Bridge Railway station when he left for Dornakal.

Rev. Azariah, the new missionary to Dornakal, reached his destination at 9:30 a.m. on Wednesday, July 28, 1909. Missionaries there were eagerly awaiting his arrival at the railway station. Children from the Mission School, both boys and girls, stood on the platform waving their flags. As soon as he disembarked from the train, missionaries welcomed him by garlanding him. from the railway station to the mission campus, the missionaries and the children went as a procession

2. Minutes of the sixth Annual General Body meeting of the IMS Society, pages 7 & 8.

singing songs and waving their flags. The children walked in the forefront of the procession. As soon as they arrived at the mission campus, they conducted a Thanksgiving prayer session in the campus chapel.

As they could not find a proper residential house on rent in Dornakal, Azariah pitched a tent and stayed there. A small hut was put up nearby to serve as their kitchen. Suviseshamuthu, whom he had brought from Palayamkottai, served as his cook. Although the facilities were few, the pastor accepted them happily.

On Sunday, August 1, 1909, Azariah delivered the sermon in the morning service. Missionary Samuel Packianathan translated the sermon into Telugu language. In the evening, they conducted a service in Tamil language for the missionaries and their families.[3]

From Monday, the pastor began his Telugu lessons. He bought a book called 'Children's Textbook' prescribed for primary grades. Within three days he completed eight lessons.

The following day, Eddy visited Dornakal. He and Azariah enjoyed exchanging pleasantries and discussing matters. Eddy left Dornakal the next day.

After learning Telugu, Azariah began to fulfill his duties. He preached in the village churches at Pirol, Meduthapalle, Thummagudem, Thotavagudem, Mangalagudem, Manukot, Choutapalle, Thetalapadu, Silveru, Pedhamupparam and Balapala. To non-Christians he preached the gospel.

Way back in October 1909, Whitehead, the Bishop in Chennai, had decided to grant the Priestly Orders to Azariah. Therefore, the pastor had to study the lessons needed for the ordination. However, owing to the visit of the then British Viceroy, the ordination ceremony was postponed to December

3. Letter to Mrs. Azariah, August 1909.

29, 1909.

We already mentioned that the Ecclesiastical jurisdiction or Diocese of the Bishop in Chennai extended to a very large area. From June 29, 1899, when he was ordained as Bishop in Chennai, and accepted that office, Whitehead felt that he needed an Assistant. Since then, he turned his attention to identifying a suitable person to assist him. Whenever he had the opportunity to meet Azariah, he often wondered, "Could this young man qualify to assist me?" When Azariah visited Whitehead to inform him of his decision to go as a missionary to Dornakal, Whitehead felt assured that the Lord was telling him, as he had told Samuel on seeing David, "Arise, anoint him, for this is he".

The day Rev. Azariah was ordained as Deacon or Assistant Pastor, Whitehead laid bare his heart to him.[4] It is hard to describe the emotions and thoughts that ran through the pastor's heart and mind when he heard Whitehead's words. We can say one thing. He pleaded with God upon his kneels, asking God, as much as he could, to introspect his life and see his own unworthiness humbling himself before God's presence, and seeking the grace of the Holy Spirit of God. He never divulged to anyone, not even to his beloved wife, the news Whitehead had broken to him. He kept it in his heart and pondered over it.

When Whitehead placed his need for an Assistant Bishop before the Bishops Council and before the Indian Provincial General Council of the Anglican Church in 1908, many supported him. At that point of time, he had not identified anyone suitable for this position. Therefore, he did not recommend anyone by name. In the days of British India, a bishop in the Anglican Church was invariably a white man. No wonder then that many missionaries coveted this position.

A few months before his ordination, Rev. Azariah received

4. Another historical data shows that it was the day prior to his ordination.

an invitation from the World Missionary Conference to attend their Conference to be held in 1910 at Edinburgh. Newly ordained Azariah and Bishop Whitehead's wife sailed by the same ship to England. Meanwhile, Mrs. Anbu Azariah along with her children had moved to Dornakal and lived there with her husband.

In April 1910, Rev. Azariah set sail for England. But, on the way, he broke his journey to visit holy places in Palestine. He reached England in the month of May and travelled to many places. At last, in June, he reached the conference venue in Edinburgh.

On June 14, the conference began at the Assembly Hall of the United Free Church. The venue that was described as the birthplace of global Christian unity was renowned in the annals of the Global church history. The Archbishop of Canterbury inaugurated the conference with his inaugural address. John Raleigh Mott presided over the other sessions. Discussions and debates were held on eight subjects as follows:[5]

1. Carrying the Gospel to all the Non-Christian World (June 15, 1910).

2. The Church in the Mission Field (June 16, 1910).

3. Education in relation to the Christianization of the National Life.

4. Missionary Message in Relation to the Non-Christian World

(June 18, 1910).

5. The Preparation of Missionaries (June 22, 1910).

6. The Home Base of Missions.

7. Missions and Governments (June 20, 1910).

5. History of the Global Christian Unification Movement' by the author, 1961,page 151.

The churches in China, Japan, Burma (Myanmar), Malaya (Malaysia), Sri Lanka, India, Madagascar, African countries, and Pacific Island were known as young churches. There was a consensus among representatives of these churches like Azariah and Harada that the topics taken up for discussions and research were important for missionary service. Therefore, these representatives paid attention to these discussions with great enthusiasm and concern. They seized opportunities to participate in the debates.

In those days, Europeans felt that they were superior and nationals from Eastern countries were inferior. This was not only the opinion of Westerners, but also that of nationals from the East. Such an inferiority complex prevailed among the Easterners. Because England ruled over India, the English openly exposed their 'we are high; you are low' mentality. Particularly, Indians in rural areas imagined that the English people were from another world. Even today, such thinking prevails among Indians. The Westerners did not hesitate to exploit this inferiority complex of Indians for their own benefit.

In the beginning of this century (early 20th Century), the spirit of Nationalism arose among Indians, and it grew. In a few years, it stirred up thirst for Independence. Not only Hindus and Muslims, but also Christians, particularly young Christians, shared this inspiration. As we mentioned earlier, Indian Christians languished under the authority of the British missionaries even in such sacred matters as the growth of Christianity. They could do nothing without first obtaining permission from Western missionaries. Many Indian Christians were frustrated by this state of affairs. The younger generation of Christians strongly felt that this situation should change at least in the Church of Lord Jesus Christ, and Western domination or hegemony should cease, and Indian Christians should be able to minister to their Lord freely and independently. Rev. Azariah was in the forefront of this young generation of Christians, and he had started the Indian Missionary Society and the National Missionary Society for this reason. When he started these societies, he laid emphasis on 'Indian money, Indian ministers, Indian methods, and Indian supervision'. His persuasive arguments won him the victory.

His debates and speeches at the Conference attained the proud heights of being 'classic' in the history of Christian unification movement. What urged him to deliver that speech was his desire that all conference delegates should know the damage caused to Church growth by this attitude of 'Westerners-Easterners and high-low'. He did not realize then that his speech may make many sad. He spoke with a firm voice and in a clear manner what was in his heart without fearing the face of man. "Western missionaries invite Indians to receive the right to sit on golden seats in heaven," he said. "But they don't ask us to sit on their plain cane chairs in the verandah of their bungalows. This is the respect white missionaries give to their fellow-Christians like us. As a result there is a deep chasm between the Western missionaries and Indian Christians. On one side, Western missionaries are proud of their higher status. On the other side, there is anger among the Indians that they are treated lowly."

"The entry of these differences has harmed the brotherhood between them. It has also obstructed the expansion of Christ's kingdom on earth. I do not ask that Westerners should pay courtesy visits to my countrymen. I do not ask for handshake or chairs or dinners. I do ask for these concessions. These concessions and more than this will come if both parties truly respect one another and love one another.

"A foreign missionary, who has come to minister to others, should first realize that he is neither a lord over the others nor a master above them. If only the foreign missionary realizes that his duty is to be a brother and a friend, the outward signs of friendship would automatically appear. The Indian Church will then rise to thank for ages those missionaries for their unselfish acts of valor. You supplied food to nourish our poor. You dared to give your bodies to be burnt for our sake. What more do we ask? Give us pure love. Give us friends."[6]

His speech ended. There was a thunderous applause. There was smile on many faces. There was joy. There was anger on other faces. Some were irritated.

The conference came to an end.

"My dear Anbu,

I think I have not written a letter to you for three or four weeks. In an hour, I have to leave for a meeting. I would like to spend the intervening time in talking a little about "Yours respectfully".[7]

In her letter to Mrs. Azariah, Mrs. Isabel Whitehead wrote the following: "I think your husband, whom you honor, should have written to you about Edinburgh. His great speech fell upon the audience like a bomb. Half the audience was delighted. The other half was furious. But we expected it. More people prayed for that speech than for any other speech. Therefore, we trust that it will be triumphant in revealing God's will and doing God's will."[8]

These words reveal how the Pastor's speech was received by the audience. Whatever the reception to the speech was,

6. G. V. Job, Op. it. Page 631.

7. Whenever Mrs. Azariah spoke to Mrs. Whitehead about her husband Rev.Azariah, like any Tamil Christian girl, she always referred to her husband respectfully using a honorific pronoun. On the contrary, Mrs. Whitehead, according to her culture, used to refer to her husband Whitehead by name. So, Mrs. Whitehead considered it strange that a wife should refer to her husband with great reverence.

8. Letter of Mrs. Isabel Whitehead, dated July 2, 1910.

it won Rev. Azariah great fame in Britain. He received invitations from London, Bristol, Oxford and other places. Journalists interviewed him.

Prior to the conference, Azariah visited Ireland. There he met many friends and addressed meetings in many towns and cities.

While returning home from Britain, he visited France and Italy. There he delighted in seeing many historical sites. He returned to India in August.

While continuing his customary missionary work in Dornakal, Rev. Azariah prepared himself for his tasks ahead by meditating on the scriptures and expanding his knowledge by reading many books. While he studied the scriptures, his mind became enriched with new ideas and expositions. In 1911, he studied the Gospel According to St. John. He wrote the thoughts that came to his mind at that time. Some excerpts from his notes follow:

Chapter 3

Event: The visit of Nicodemus.

The State without Christ **Through Christ**

- Man cannot see God's kingdom.1. The new rebirth.
- Man cannot enter God's kingdom 2. Eternal Life.
- Man cannot receive Eternal Life3. No judgment / condemnation.
- Man under judgment / condemnation. 4. Obtain salvation.

Another chapter

Chapter 10

The State without Christ		With Christ	
1.	Sheep without shepherd.	1.	Christ, the Good Shepherd.
2.	Led by thieves.	2.	He goes before us.
3.	False shepherd flees when wolf comes.	3.	He calls us by name.
4.	People's hatred.	4.	Knowing His voice.
5.	Picking up stones to throw.	5.	Abundant Life.
6.	Opposition to the truth.	6.	He knows those who are His.
		7.	Known by those who are His.
		8.	The One Who gives His life.
		9.	Safety & Salvation in Him.

Another Chapter

Chapter 13

Event: The Last Supper and Washing the Disciples Feet.

The State without Christ		With Christ	
1.	No part with God.	1.	Life washed by Christ.
2.	Betraying God.	2.	Life of humility and humble service.
		3.	Life full of good works.
		4.	Life full of love.

In this manner he studied all the chapters of the book by writing notes and compiling them.[9] In the same way, he worked with other books.

While Rev. Azariah was engrossed in his service and studies,

Bishop Whitehead was busy executing his plans. According to the then prevalent rules, if a new Diocese was to be created or a new bishop was to be ordained, the Central Government, on the recommendation of the Provincial Government, must apply to the British Parliament. After their consent, the British Viceroy-Governor General in India must grant his consent too. With the permission of the Metropolitan in Calcutta (now Kolkata) Copleston, Whitehead applied to the Government. In his application he wrote that he needed an Assistant Bishop, who should also become the Bishop in Dornakal once the Dornakal Diocese is delineated and bifurcated from the Chennai Diocese. In the course of time, he received the necessary approval of the government and the Viceroy / Governor-General.

In February 1912, it was declared that V. S. Azariah, one of the missionaries of the Indian Missionary Society in Dornakal, has been chosen to be ordained as the Bishop in Dornakal and Assistant Bishop to the Bishop in Chennai.

As soon as the Official Declaration was promulgated, many wrote to the Metropolitan opposing Azariah's nomination as Bishop. Here we give a gist of the content of such letters: 'How can European missionaries serve under an Indian? What disgrace to Western Superiority! How can English pastors endure the disgrace of addressing an Indian Bishop as My Lord? No, never! We should not let this thing come to pass. If Azariah has to be made a Bishop, then let him be an Assistant Bishop. It is not right to grant him, an Indian, the privilege of sitting along with English bishops. If he is granted a separate Diocese of his own, then he will get this privilege and dignity. Therefore, the Diocese of Dornakal should not be formed. If the Metropolitan disregards such opposition, then it would harm missionary work. Therefore, he should act carefully to prevent such a situation from arising.'

One suggestion said, "If an Indian has to be ordained as bishop, then let them find an Indian province where no

British pastor serves under the Indian government's Indian Ecclesiastical Department. Let them form a Diocese in such a province, and give it to him."

What Christian humility of the English missionaries! An achievement in line with their teaching! Neither Whitehead nor Copleston feared this ripple of protests cared for it. No pastor belonging to the Government's Ecclesiastical Department served in the areas falling under the proposed Dornakal Diocese. So the protesters were somewhat satisfied that the two bishops had accepted at least one of ideas of the protesters.

Apart from the missionaries, there were others who protested. Some British officers, businessmen and others wrote various petitions, either jointly or individually, to the Metropolitan Copleston and other bishops, to the Chennai Governor, Viceroy and other government heads, and the Secretary of State for India. The last three of them returned the petitions to the petitioners.

Let it be! The hegemonic arrogance and dictatorial pride of the ruling class of the erstwhile British could not tolerate an Indian occupying a high position in his own church in his own country. Their action was like a Venetian Blind before their eyes, blocking their vision. This is how we, who live today, understand it.

Even some Indians could not tolerate one of their own brothers attain a high position, and that too, in Christian ministry. They also opposed it either individually or sometimes in unison with the English. Should we laugh at this situation or cry over it? The Christian community in Chennai conveyed their opposition. Various reasons were cited. We will look into them later. Many residents of Chennai did not know Azariah. They had no legitimate rights over him except for the fact that he was an Indian.

Alas! The news that Azariah was going to be consecrated as Bishop was bitter even to his own Tirunelveli Christians. They prepared a long petition signed by 1,100 persons, and sent it to the Metropolitan and Whitehead.[10] How dare that a black man (Azariah's skin color was indeed black) thinks that he can attain a position that until then was occupied by white men alone. Those 1,100 persons and many others could not even imagine that a black man could occupy a position that rightfully belonged to white people because for generations it was the white people who led and governed our churches and occupied leadership positions in the Church, and sat on the high seats during lent or other annual religious festivals. The white people were praised and held up like angels before Indian Christians. How, then, can a black Indian, even if he was one of their own men, occupy the position of a Bishop? It is not possible to eradicate something that was ingrained in their blood. Therefore, let's not cry! Let's not laugh!

Some of the points raised by Azariah's European, Indian and Tirunelveli opponents were:

• Azariah was young. There were many who were older than him.

• He did not have high secular education or theological education.

• He was acquainted more with non-Anglican church people, and

trained by them. Therefore, he cannot be accepted as a Churchman.

• In his social life, he did not belong to a high caste.

• There were many who were godlier and holier than him.[11]

Despite so much opposition, there were many Europeans

10. Madras Mail 1912 – Date cut off.

11. An Article on the objectors' points of view by an Indian Christian in "United India & Native States" dated January 4, 1913.

(not missionaries), Indian Christians and Tirunelveli church members who welcomed him. Church leaders in Europe, America and Britain praised Whitehead. Indian church leaders as well as Hindu leaders praised Copleston and Whitehead as visionaries.

The day was drawing near for Rev. Azariah to become Bishop. It was notified that this distinguished Ordination ceremony would take place on December 29, 1912,[12] at St. Paul's Cathedral in Calcutta (Kolkata). A lot of preparations for this ceremony were being carried on in Dornakal, Chennai and Calcutta. Azariah and his wife Anbu prepared themselves by kneeling down and praying. Copleston sent the following prayer to be prayed in all Anglican churches throughout India.

> "Almighty Father, you have purchased the Church by the priceless precious blood of your dear Son. Pour out your heavenly blessing upon your servant Vedhanayagam Samuel Azariah whom you have called to be Bishop of that church. May your Holy Spirit mature him and adorn him with the necessary gifts. May your gospel spread across this Indian nation without any obstacle and be glorified! May your holy kingdom be firmly established! Grant us the grace that all of us may serve you unitedly through prayer, counsel, and humble service. We pray through our Lord Jesus Christ. Amen."

Meanwhile, those who opposed the ordination of Rev. Azariah spread the news stressing that Azariah would serve only as an Assistant Bishop performing the duties of the Bishop whenever the Bishop was absent. When he came to know this, Copleston, in order to obliterate that fake news, immediately issued a notification as follows: "It is not correct to say that Azariah is the Assistant Bishop in Chennai. He is not only

12. The third anniversary day of Azariah's ordination as pastor.

Assistant Bishop in Chennai, but also has a small Diocese for himself. In this regard, he is like the Bishop in Tirunelveli and the Bishop in Chota Nagpur. He is a member of the Episcopal Synod. In this respect, he is a Diocesan Bishop as well as an Assistant Bishop having oversight of Indian churches falling in a large part of the Chennai Diocese. It is not correct to say that he is the first Indian Bishop; for the Syrian Church in Malabar has been having Indian bishops for centuries. But, Azariah is the first Indian member of the Anglican Church to be ordained as Bishop."[13]

Many Tirunelveli Christians assembled at the Palayamkottai Centenary Hall. Azariah, the Nellai Christian pastor and a Missionary of Tirunelveli Indian Missionary Society, the Society that birthed the Dornakal churches through its missionary work, was going to be consecrated as the Dornakal Bishop. Tirunelveli Christians met at the Centenary Hall to discuss in what ways they could honor him. They decided to raise Rs.1,000 from Nellai Christians living in South India,Sri Lanka, Malaya (Malaysia), Burma (Myanmar), and other places. With this money, they planned to get a Pastoral Staff made, and get a Commendation Message printed. This message would be read during his ordination ceremony, and the staff would be gifted to him. That was their plan. To execute their plans, they formed a powerful Executive Committee. Mr. A. S. Appasamy, a renowned lawyer and a close friend of Rev. Azariah and organizer of the Indian Missionary Society, was appointed as the President of the Committee. Mr. G.Devadason, a teacher, who later became a pastor and a leader among Nellai pastors, was appointed as the Committee Secretary. Nellai Christians donated enthusiastically for this purpose. All over Nellai, people were united in joy and enthusiasm (except, perhaps, in the hearts of the 1,100 protestors).

At 8:00 a.m. on December 29, 1912, many dignitaries and

13. The Statesman, Calcutta August 9, 1912.

others gathered in St. Paul's Cathedral in Calcutta (Kolkata). They walked in procession into the Cathedral in this order: the choir, the Cathedral staff, pastors, Cathedral pastors, Rev. Azariah, two of his chaplains; the bishops in Lucknow, Rangoon (Yangon), Ranchi (Chota Nagpur), Travancore-Kochi, Tirunelveli, Nagpur, Colombo, Lahore, Bombay (Mumbai) and Chennai with their respective chaplains; crucifer, the Registrar of Calcutta Diocese, the first chaplain of the Metropolitan, the Metropolitan himself, and his second chaplain. After they had been seated in their respective seats, the Metropolitan started the Holy Communion service. The Bombay Bishop read the designated passage in Acts 20: 17 instead of the regular reading from an Epistle. The Chennai Bishop read the Gospel reading from Matthew 28: 18. Rev. Canon E. Sell, Secretary of the Madras Corresponding Committee of the CMS delivered a valuable sermon based on Hebrew 3: 14-19. After the sermon, the Bishop in Chennai and the Bishop in Tirunelveli set Azariah before the Metropolitan. The service was held in this order: Reading of the chapter on Ordination, taking the oath of office, Congregational prayer, singing of the Litany, Question and Answer Session, donning the liturgical vestments of a Bishop, and congregational singing. Then, as Azariah knelt before the Communion table, they sang with great reverence the hymn, "Come, Holy Spirit, Descend on us!" After the Metropolitan prayed, he consecrated Rev. Azariah as Bishop by the laying on of hands and presentation of the Hoy Bible.

The Holy Communion service continued. The Bishop in Colombo, the Bishop in Chennai, and the Bishop in Bombay assisted the Metropolitan in the distribution of the Bread and the Cup. At last, the Metropolitan pronounced the Benediction. They adjourned in a procession in the same order in which they came in. This time, however, the new Bishop accompanied the Metropolitan.

The same evening, the Nellai Christians who had come from all over India, Burma (Myanmar), Sri Lanka and other places formally read their 'Courtesy Reception Message' thanking the Metropolitan and Bishop Whitehead. The Metropolitan responded by greeting Azariah, saying, "Azariah has become a pucca (proper) Bishop." "This is a day of great joy in his life," said Whitehead. "Azariah's ordination as a Bishop holds a special place among all the special occasions in the history of the Indian Church, in the centuries following the ordination of India's first Bishop in 1815. After the reading of the 'formal Document of Greetings', Nellai Christians gifted a specially made Bishop's Staff, which was a symbol of their love'. In response to their request, Bishop Azariah lovingly received the formal document encased in a silver casket, and 'the Bishop's Staff'. Then he thanked them and all the Nellai Christians. He prayed and blessed them.

All bishops who had come for the ordination participated in this celebration. Dornakal missionaries gifted Bishop Azariah with a Bishop's ring. The Bishop in Chennai was happy to gift his friend a beautiful Pectoral Cross. Members of the NMS Society presented him small silver cups to be used in the distribution of the wine or grape juice during the Holy Communion. The man who read 'the Document of Greetings' of the Nellai Christians and encased it in the casket was the lawyer Paul Appasamy, who later was elevated to the position of a Judge.

Many photographs were taken on the occasion. One photograph showed Bishop Azariah with all the other bishops. Another snap showed him with his wife, his children and the Nellai Christians. There was one marked difference in his appearance before he became a Bishop and his appearance on the day of his ordination and thereafter. Before he became a Bishop he sported a thick, bushy moustache! But on the day of his ordination, he had removed it.

CHAPTER 5

AZARIAH, THE BISHOP

"…he is a chosen vessel unto me." Acts 9: 15.

"Expect great things from God; attempt great things for God," said William Carey, and based on this his motto, he had started a great missionary movement, and was popularly known as 'the Father of Modern Missions'. In Serampore, which was Carey's field of work, the All India Christian Students Convention was being held in Serampore the week Azariah was consecrated as Bishop. Azariah had not forgotten YMCA and other youth organizations that had made him rise to this level. Because he had been serving as Vice-President of the YMCA, and because he had received special invitation to attend the convention, Azariah took part in the convention the very next day following his ordination. He helped to make the convention successful. That day, he performed a service that became a clear precursor to and a prophetic act for the great ministry that he was to fulfill all his life. In the same place by the banks of River Hooghly, where Dr. William Carey had baptized the first-fruit of his labors, Krishna Pal, who had surrendered to Christ and had joined the church, in the same spot Bishop Azariah baptized two young men on December 31, 1912, three days after his ordination as Bishop. He had 'the blessed privilege of bringing some to the flock', which was his first ministry as Bishop. Both the baptized men were educated: one of them, a Brahmin, was studying for his Master's degree. About 300 persons took part in that service. The Principal of Bishop's College in Kolkata, Rev. Lee, assisted Bishop Azariah in that service. International Christian leaders, who attended the Convention and also the All India Centenary Missionary conference, particularly the Scholar John Raleigh Mott, witnessed the baptism service and blessed the new Christians. Although Dr. Urquehart, a missionary of the Scotland Episcopal Church, and G. S. Eddy, a YMCA missionary and Bishop Azariah's friend, both had been instrumental in leading Azariah to Christ, both of them became members of the Anglican Church.[1]

The first missionary Dr. Carey, who had spent his body, substance and spirit in the work of making Indians as Christ's slaves, baptized his first fruits and offered them to the Lord. By giving the same kind of immersion baptism by the banks of River Hooghly to a Brahmin man and another man, the first Indian Anglican Bishop made them children of his God. Azariah, who had dedicated himself to the kind of missionary work that Carey had started, by this baptism proclaimed prophetically that he was going to lead thousands of people in Andhra to Christ and bring them into the Church through baptism. Moreover, several missionary societies were formed to continue the great missionary work that Carey had started, and also to reap the manifold benefits from it. One such Missionary Society was the CMS that had birthed its precious son Bishop Azariah. It was as if this baptism ceremony was showing that the Lord had sealed him as "a chosen vessel unto me".

On January 8, 1913, Bishop Azariah returned to Dornakal. People of that new Diocese accorded him a warm welcome. Was not that day a remarkable day in Indian history? In the divine service held with great devotion in the Dornakal church, India's first Indian bishop occupied his Bishop's seat. In the history of the Indian Church, a new diocese under an Indian

1. The Statesman, Calcutta, January 1, 1913.

bishop was formed. It was the beginning of a new chapter.

The diocese was small. There were six Telugu-speaking pastors. There were 172 workers serving the churches. There were 8,000 Christians. This number includes about 1,500 new Christians who were the fruits of the Indian Missionary Society. Only a few CMS churches, which were outside the Manukot taluk (sub-division), were added to this new diocese. But, other Anglican pastorates in Andhra continued to be under the Bishop in Chennai. As an Assistant Bishop to the Bishop in Chennai, Azariah kept fulfilling his duties as a bishop in Chennai diocese too as and when needed.

From the beginning, Azariah set out to work vigorously for the development of his diocese. The mission campus West of Dornakal Railway Station was in many ways lacking facilities for the ministry and the ministry workers. Therefore, he bought a large piece of land to the East of the Railway Station near a hillock.

In the old campus he built a solid, but small, church building. It was not in the Bishop's thought to make it a permanent church. Nevertheless, it served as a church for 25 years until the Cathedral was built.

In the course of time, he built a small house for himself, houses for missionaries, and houses for mission workers, apart from school buildings and other buildings. Until 'the bishop's palace' was built, he lived in the small house that he had just built.

What he did in Dornakal, he also did in other Christian villages: buying large plots of land, and building houses for mission workers, churches, and other necessary buildings. He gave a large part of the remaining money to poor members of the village churches for their sustenance. In some of these villages, he made arrangements for the mission workers to cultivate these plots of land and generate some income, while they continued to do their church ministry. Examples of such churches were Meduthapalle, Choutapalle and Modhukulagudem. [2]

In 1912, Azariah called Mr. Manonmani and appointed him as Writer or Clerk at the Diocesan office. Apart from this his regular job, he was given the task of purchasing plots of land and apportioning these among poor Christians for cultivation, and facilitating their sustenance by means of cultivation.

In 1919, when some poor people in Ahmednagar became Christians, they were persecuted by high caste people. People who had become Christians came from the low Mala caste, who had been traditionally working as farm laborers on agricultural farms belonging to high caste landlords. Now the landlord did not permit the Mala people to cultivate lands or work as 'coolies' (manual laborers earning daily wages). They also prevented low caste people from burying the corpses of their dear ones in their villages. Poor Christians respectfully addressed Bishop Azariah as 'thanrigaru' (respected father), poured out their complaint to him, and tearfully sought his help. He did what was needed to wipe out their tears and troubles. He bought 130 acres of land with the help of Whitehead, the Bishop in Chennai. With Manonmani's help, he got the new Christians settled on this land. He named the new settlement as 'Vedhanayagapuram' in memory of his father.

In the same year 1919, white corn famine struck Mupparam area. Many parents sold their children as they could not feed them, and survived with that money. Some persons died. Bishop Azariah and IMS missionary Rev. J. Iyadurai took great efforts to obtain help from the government for the famine-affected people. In addition, they saved many

2. 'Fifty years of Indian Missionary Society Tirunelveli', in Telugu, by Rev. K.Luke in manuscripts. Translated into Tamil by I. V. Manuel Raj.

from the ravages of the famine by giving them jobs in the building project of the Dornakal Cathedral. The Bishop also saved lives by buying rice from Burma (Myanmar) with the help of the government, and selling them, with Rev. Iyadurai's help, at a very low price of one rupee for six seers (about one kilogram) of rice. Despite this, many went to Dornakal and bowed before Azariah requesting him with tears to save them. He did whatever he could to satisfy their hunger. Apart from this, he also settled them in Kreedapuram (Crown village) by the slopes of a hillock near the Dornakal Mission Campus, and sustained them. He named the village as 'Crown Village' in memory of the coronation of King George V. The timely help rendered by the Bishop and mission servants helped the 'Pallam' community people in Mulakanoor village to be delivered from their famine-time sorrows. Many of them saw Christ's love evident in these actions, and joined the Church in 1923. A few churches like the Vanthadupula Church illustrate the truth of this statement.

The service rendered by the bishop to sustain and preserve the poor paved the way for them to know in reality that he was their 'father', and also to listen to his words out of affection. All through his life he never hesitated to grant such Christian benefits to people and preserve them. If we begin to write in detail all what he did, this book cannot contain them. It is enough to point out a few of them:

Panthampalle village. The people belonged to the Madiga caste, a low caste. They were poor. They were sad and distressed unable to bear their heavy burden of debts. The moneylender was an upper caste man. He threatened his debtors and deceived them by grabbing their dry and wet lands. He oppressed them. The poor were helpless. Rev. Sreenivasan came to know about this. He, with the Bishop's help and influence, put down the high-handed behavior of the rich moneylender. He made the moneylender agree to a settlement by which the poor debtors would repay their loans over a period of four or five years in easy installments. In 1926, the Bishop thus liberated them.

Nagaram: A small town owned by a wealthy landlord. He was a heartless man. He treated people under his control as animals. He treated both low caste people and middle caste people harshly. When the middle caste people, the Shudras, opposed him, he started treating them more severely than before. Those poor, oppressed people looked for someone to help them. Finally, they approached Rev. M. P. Israel, a Telugu pastor, and through him poured out their sorrows to the Bishop. They came to the Bishop seeking deliverance from worldly distresses, but the hope that he gave them was something greater. It was about deliverance that the Savior Jesus offers from Satan who is far crueler than the landlord.

When they heard the Christian gospel from him, enthusiastically they showed interest in knowing more about it. The Bishop sent the right missionaries who could proclaim the gospel to them in a way they could understand it. Many of them from the Shudra communities, who were simple people, believed and were baptized. They placed their faith in the gospel and were baptized. Will the landlord still (in 1937) dare to oppress them?

If new Christians suffered from trouble and distress from upper caste people, wealthy people and landlords, for the sole reason that they knew Christ, put their faith in Him, and joined the church, then they sought the Bishop's aid. But the Bishop did not go at once to their aid. "Their faith must be purified by refining, and glow," said Azariah, explaining his policy. "They should endure tests and trials. The world must realize that those people did not take refuge in Lord Christ for worldly advancement or for the protection given by the Mission. That will be their witness that glorifies their Savior."

Sankesu: In this village, upper caste people caused terrible tribulation to Christians belonging to the '*puttalaruthi*' and '*vaddera*' sub-groups of 'Yerukula' community (1916), while the entire village of **Raavirala** did the same to the Christians belonging to the 'Yerukala' community (1917). During 1922, local landlords treated the 'Mala' Christians in **Ahmednagar Punjer** terribly, while Hindus in **Thopalagudem** troubled the '*kammaala*' Christians. The inhabitants of **Dodla** village troubled 'Mala' Christians (1928). The wealthy people of **Narasimhulapeta** (Telangana) ill-treated the 'Mala' and 'Dhaalaali' Christians (1931). The zamindars (landlords) of Nagaram caused terrible tribulation to the Shudra Christians (1935, 1937). This news was reported by the Indian Missionary Society within their areas of operation. Across the diocese, many such incidents were reported. In all these incidents, the Bishop rendered suitable help and protected the people.

As mentioned earlier, whenever such miseries happened, the Bishop waited patiently for a little time, but when it appeared that the persecuted Christians were no longer able to endure the persecution, he sent missionaries or other ministers to the victims with orders to ameliorate their sufferings. If they could not get it done, then the Bishop himself would intervene using his authority and influence to protect the people. If he could not do it, then he would seek assistance from the government, or he may re-settle the victims in a Christian community. We already looked at one or two examples of such action from his history. Among the notable missionaries who received orders from the Bishop and ameliorated people's suffering were Rev. I. J. Iyyadurai, Rev. Jel Knight, Rev. Sreenivasan, Rev. D. Devasahayam and Rev. M. P. Israel.

"For a Christian, bearing suffering is witnessing for the Lord," said the bishop stressing his teaching. "Just enduring suffering alone cannot become an excellent witness. It is useful only if true Christian living goes along with endurance." Just one mission field shows the manifold benefits of this emphatic teaching. But we see that this was the case in other areas too.

In **Raavirala** village, Rev. Devasahayam proclaimed the gospel and led many people from the Yerukula community to the knowledge of the Redeemer. On seeing these people join the Christian Church, the local Hindu people were enraged. Earlier, Yerukula people had been living by committing horrible crimes like robbery, thefts and banditry. Therefore, the government and the police had placed restrictions and rules governing this community. As a result, this community became the target of public's hatred, derision and loathing. After becoming Christians, their lifestyle changed completely. "Old things have passed away; behold, all things have become new" (II Corinthians 5: 17). They began to live upright Christian lives, showing deep devotion and faith in Lord Jesus Christ, and enduring the afflictions that befell them. They became meek, humble and loving. This transformation in their lives earned them their enemies' sympathy and appreciation. Troubles ceased, and peace prevailed. Moreover, other Yerukula people were attracted by these newly transformed Yerukulas. On seeing their own Yerukula people in Raavirala village give up their traditional cruel and evil practices, and adopt lives of good conduct, thus earning the respect and honor of the society, Yerukulas from **Sankesu** (1916), **Silukodu, Rajoma, Koruvi, Gundarathimadugu,** and **Thodalagudem** villages also, in course of time, sought the religion of Christ, joined the Church, and became the people of God.

On observing the transformed lives of the 'Mala' Christians in **Sriramagiri**, which was in stark contrast to their past lives, and seeing how they now lived as Christians with true peace and joy, the others came to Lord Jesus Who was the cause of this change, and they joined the Church. Among them were the Malas from **Inkurthi** village (1924). The noble and upright lives of the church members in **Mangalagudem** and **Polisettigudem** led the people of **Madholigudem** village to the Savior (1923). The holiness of the people of **Kesamudram** Church led to the establishment of the

Upparapalle Church (1927). These people who rejoiced in the Lord's gracious blessing became evangelists proclaiming to others the truth that they discovered. The excellent lives of the new Christians in **Pochannapalle** led to the formation of the **Gundamraasipalle** Church (1930). The radiance of the good conduct of the **Kamalapuram** Church was instrumental in starting a new church in **Krotha Kamalapuram** (1932). The light that shone in the holy lives of **Thirumalaipalayam** Christians enabled people to find Christ and form a church in **Chinthalapalle**. The excellent upright lives of Christians in **Sriramagiri** caused another church to open, this time in **Munakaliveedu**, which comprised of Yerukulas. Because a church was started in **Korudhapeta**, later a church in **Seethapeta** was born. The Mala church in **Payanampalle** was an offering from **Meduthapalle** Christians. **Vaddera** church people who settled down in **Rajole** formed the Yerukula church. The church that Christ established in **Subraveedu** village had seventy low-caste people, whose transformed lives, won two young men from the upper-caste community that had derided low-caste Christians. These young men turned into warriors of Lord Jesus Christ. There was one man in **Dodla** village who became a Christian. He endured all suffering and obstacles, and served free of cost the church that comprised of Mala people who had become Christ's slaves, a magnificent history of how upper-caste people were attracted. Many were the pains suffered by the church in **Sollakalavi** village. But they maintained patience, and more patience, to the extent that it frustrated their enemies. What brought them pride ultimately? It was the excellence of getting their oppressors taste the joy of the love of Lord Jesus Christ (1926).

"The proclamation of the gospel is a service to be continually done by missionaries, church ministers and pastors," said Bishop Azariah, emphasizing these facts repeatedly in his sermons to the ministers. "Lay people in the Church should carry Lord Jesus Christ in them, but they are also responsible to proclaim, along with the ministers, the truth which they had found and experienced." Although Azariah was continually involved in many, multifarious ministries more than many other bishops in India, he personally paid more attention to the fundamental ministry of proclaiming the gospel. Whether riding a bicycle or sitting in an ox-drawn cart, he travelled in forests overrun with wild animals and in hot regions, in extremes of climate. During the day, he visited churches; by night he travelled; in the evenings, he preached the gospel. This was his practice. In proclaiming the gospel, he sought for 'dry areas' and places where the opposition to the gospel was great, and personally visited such places to accomplish his 'direct service'. **Thirumalapalem** village greatly opposed the gospel. It was a 'dry place'. Ministers of the Indian Missionary Society did not give up. It was to such a hard place that Rev. Devasahayam eventually invited the Bishop. **Thirumalapuram** heeded the sweet words of the Bishop, and listened to the truth that he spoke, and submitted to God. Until this day, it remains a fertile church. We already saw how the holy life of its church members led **Chinthalapalle** to the love of the Lord.

We already mentioned that missionaries and catechists, being the church's ministers, considered proclamation of the gospel as their foremost duty. If we begin to write about all of them, there would be no sufficient space here. Nevertheless, we will mention a few of them.

Rev. Devashayam and his co-workers: Jayaram Yerukula church, Raavirala Yerukula church, Thirumalapalem, Parvathigiri, and many others.

Rev. Sreenivasan and his co-workers: Neradai, Korukondapalle, Komatipalle, Kesamudram and others.

Rev. Iyadurai and his co-workers: Potlada, Ellampeta Korandalar, Kotapattilar church, Kothapalle, Bommakkal, Ramannagudem Jungamar Church, Thandalapalle,

Chillamcherla, and many others. It was Rev. Iyadurai who formed the Mupparam pastorate.

We have given here briefly just a small part of the work of a few missionaries. It is impossible to write more on the work done by other missionaries, pastors and catechists, and the fruits they bore. The ministry of Dornakal Indian Missionary Society forms a small part of the entire ministry done across the diocese. If that small part of the ministry is so great, how many times greater would have been the ministry accomplished by S.P.G., C.M.S. and other larger missions across the diocese. A large component of the bishop's entire administrative duty, his responsibility to guide the affairs of the diocese, and the burden of management, must have been apportioned to 'the Department of Gospel Ministry'!

The following report shows the results of the ministry of the Dornakal Indian Missionary Society. It points to its growth with the active support of Bishop Azariah.[3]

	1915	**1925**	**1935**	**1945**
Persons Baptized	1035	2479	6112	10001
Prepared for Baptism	912	1354	3472	2042
Communicant Members	179	438	993	1178
Churches	56	100	137	143
Church Ministers	41	40	38	38
Boarding School Students	62	67	70	69

In 1945, there were 12,043 Christians including those who were baptized and those being prepared for baptism. There were almost 2,40,000 Christians across the whole diocese. Among them, those who joined the Church as a result of the ministry of the Indian Missionary Society amounted to about five percent. You may guess how great the rich experience of the Bishop's ministry might have been.

Some may complain that Bishop Azariah and his assistants, like the 19th century missionaries, brought the basest and downtrodden people into the Church. His teaching in this matter was very similar to the teaching of Lord Jesus Christ Who came to heal sinners and the notorious tax-collectors. "Out of India's population of 320 million people, only four million are Christians," said Azariah. "A majority of Indian Christians are downtrodden people. In the nature of Jesus Christ, it was these oppressed and despicable ones who were attractive to Him. We cannot offer a more magnificent service to the religion of Christ than to make the downtrodden people equal in status to the upper caste people."[4]

Upper-caste people, who observed the change in heart and improvement in good conduct and pious behavior of the downtrodden people in Dornakal diocese, were all in praise and appreciation. And they sent messengers to the bishop requesting him 'to invite the low-caste people in their villages to the Christ Church'. "Upper caste Hindus often visit me and request me to bring Christianity to their village," said Azariah in his address to churches in New Zealand. "Upper caste people unhesitatingly testified of the good works Christianity has done among 'the untouchables', the lowest-caste people. Nine out of ten Christians in the Telugu speaking areas hailed from the lower castes. I was bewildered by the pace at which the low caste people joined the Church. Village after village joined the Church. Fifty out of a hundred persons attended the daily morning church service. Ninety persons attend the Sunday church service. 'Come and help us' is the cry of Indians to you. They seek your help to train ministers able to proclaim the gospel and to shepherd the believers."[5]

---

4. From an address Bishop Azariah gave at the Cathedral in Christchurch, New Zealand, during his visit. Date not presented.
5. Ibid

From the data given above regarding the growth of the work of the Indian Missionary Society, it is evident that from 1915 to 1945 there was no rise in the number of church ministers from Telugu speaking areas. It is also evident that the number of boarding school boys and girls remained stagnant. The same situation prevailed in other parts of the diocese too!

When Azariah was the General Secretary of the Indian Missionary Society, its first missionary Samuel Packianathan established the Dornakal Boarding School. His younger brother Solomon Packianathan, its third missionary, became its manager from 1908, and stabilized the school. Bishop Azariah selected some of its students and put them in the CMS School at Khammamedu. Soon after they completed their school studies, he got them involved in Teaching as well as in church and evangelistic ministries. From 1919 onwards, he took the outstanding students who had completed Form III in Khammamedu, and put some of them in Nandyal High School and the others in the Noble High School at Machilipatnam so that they could receive Higher Education. Some of them became missionaries. Those who completed Form III schooling were sent to be trained by Rev. Samuel Packianathan in homiletics (preaching) and other church ministries at Dornakal School. From 1923, others were sent to Rev. S. S. Subbiah for similar training. Although the Bishop made such arrangements for their training, owing to time constraints he could not directly train church servants and ministers needed by the fast-growing churches. This situation prevailed not only in the mission areas of the Indian Missionary Society, but also in other mission areas. The reason for this shortcoming could be that Azariah did not follow an excellent principle followed by the Tirunelveli missions. The early missionaries from SPCK, CMS and SPG missions operating in Tirunelveli followed the good practice of starting Primary Schools in churches. By this method, most of the members of the Church became literate within one or two generations. The pastors established boarding schools for boys and girls in villages in their Circle of operation. Here they admitted boys and girls who had excelled in their education in Grade III, and gave them education up to Form III (equal to Grade VIII). From among them, they chose some who excelled in academic studies as well as good conduct, and put them in seminaries at Palayamkottai and Sawyerpuram. The girls were admitted in Teacher Training institutions at Palayamkottai and Nazareth. After they passed out, both boys and girls were appointed to serve in churches or as teachers in schools. Thus they prepared many persons to serve as missionaries not only in their own mission areas, but also in mission areas as far away as Madurai, Tiruchi and the Nilgiris districts. But this method was not adopted in the Dornakal area (as far as we know, at least, not in the mission areas of the Indian Missionary Society). Many reasons may be attributed to this, such as lack of facilities or lackadaisical attitude of the local people. Whatever the reason, this was the situation.

In 1956, in his book on church history, Rev. K. Luke had outlined two painful causes for this situation: (i) 'No minister could be appointed in the church for want of ministers.' (ii) 'There are merely five persons or ten persons or fourteen persons in this church who are literate enough to read the Bible in their own language.' There were other causes too. What other reason than the fact that there were no schools in villages? According to the 1945 Census, there were only about 150 village schools in the diocesan jurisdiction, although there were more than 2,000 churches and 240,000 Christians in this diocese.

The Telugu-speaking Christians praise the Bishop highly, but they have one grouse against him. "The Father thought that it was sufficient to train the poor Christians in cottage industries like weaving, leather craft, carpentry, a little farming and poultry-keeping," they said. "He did not like us to pursue undergraduate studies. He did not permit the Dornakal School to be upgraded to above or beyond Form III." Whether this grouse was true or false, it is natural for us to feel sorry that this generation thought so.

Centuries ago, around the year 1870, Christians belonging to Tirunelveli CMS and SPG missions also thought in this manner. And it was not without a proper reason. All CMS missionaries and all SPG missionaries (except Anderson in Sawyerpuram) felt that there was no need for Tirunelveli Christians to study beyond Form III. People admitted Hindu and Muslim students in the English medium high schools that the Missions had started. After Nellai Christians became aware of this and protested, only then were their children admitted in the English medium high schools. Had they not protested in this manner, neither the high schools run by Palayamkottai CMS, Srivilliputhur CMS, Meignanapuram CMS, Nazareth SPG, Sawyerpuram SPG and Ramanathapuram SPG, or the Tirunelveli C.M. College, Palayamkottai Sarah Tucker College, and Sawyerpuram SPG College (including the future Caldwell College in Tuticorin) would not have come into existence. We would not have got scholars like Azariah so easily.

One undeniable fact is that the Bishop succeeded in giving the Dornakal Christians excellent training that they mature in Christian faith, Christian code of conduct, and Christian knowledge, to the end that they may become true witnesses of their Savior by word and by deeds in their lives.

There is another good thing which Bishop Azariah superbly adopted from the history of the Tirunelveli Church. As soon as a Christian church is formed in a village, missionaries in Tirunelveli built a small church building there, and conducted daily morning and evening church service that missionaries regularly attended. This was a valuable practice that they had emphasized. Azariah adopted this practice in Dornakal

Diocese too. He insisted that every community – the low-caste Mala, Madiga, Manthular, Jungmer, and Yerukular – as well as the upper caste Chetty or Reddy ought to build for themselves churches. To start with, they raised structures made of coconut leaves. In course of time, buildings made of lime-plastered or stucco walls and tiled roofs turned into large churches.

It is very necessary to train efficient pastors who could administer the Holy Sacraments, and shepherd the Church. How can we ever imagine that Azariah, who had set up two missions when he was YMCA secretary and concuded that they must be Indianized, would depend upon Western pastors to serve in his diocese? Therefore, very soon, in 1921, he planned to set up a Pastoral Training Institute, and in 1921 he executed his plan.

From the time he set up the Pastoral Training Institute, he evinced interest in it all through his lifetime. As long as he lived in Dornakal, he taught at the Institute for at least two hours every day, an hour in the morning and an hour in the evening, except for the days he was travelling. To assist him in this work, he transferred Rev. A. B. Elliot to Dornakal. Elliot had served superbly as the first CMS missionary from 1913 at Khammamedu, and had earned a good report. Elliot served as the Principal of this new Institute and greatly helped the Bishop in the making of many excellent pastors.

In 1929, buildings needed for the Institute were constructed. Student family quarters were built to enable students to reside in the campus with their families. Fletcher Hall[6] was built in the first floor to serve as a chapel, while the ground floor served as a classroom.

Apart from Elliot, other missionaries like Rev. F. F.

6. It was named after Ms. Fletcher who had donated a thousand British pounds when the Bishop visited England. This money was used for building the hall.

Gladstone and Indian pastors also labored in the construction work from time to time. They worked in a manner that pleased the Bishop. In the course of time that Institute developed into a Bible College that prepared pastors needed for the Church in Andhra.

Mrs. Anbu Azariah conducted classes for the wives of the pastoral students. This way, she helped every one of them to lend able support each one to her husband in his ministry.

For a long time, the Bishop had desired to have a medical clinic opened at Dornakal. But he had no resources for it. Therefore, whenever he travelled abroad, he raised the needed money. And, in 1923, he opened the newly built Dornakal Mission Medical Center. The medical doctor he appointed was Dr. J. S. Williams, who had a qualified Licentiate in Medical Practice (LMP). He was the elder son of Mr. Jacob who had served for some time as a missionary of the Indian Missionary Society. Dr. Williams already ran his own medical clinic in Dornakal. After he became a Mission Doctor he focused on the mission work and worked hard for its development. The inspiration and encouragement that the Bishop gave him was indeed great. Bishop Whitehead, Bishop in Chennai, who knew well the good work done by the medical clinic, donated some money. In 1929, Azariah got a building built with this money. He named the newly built Medical Center as 'Bishop Whitehead Medical Center', and blessed it. In appreciation of the good work done by the Medical Center, the Nizam government donated about Rs.3,000 as assistance. In 1943, Azariah committed the responsibility of running the Medical Center to the Indian Missionary Society. He did this with the intention of obtaining permanent support to run the Center. The Indian Missionary Society also wholeheartedly accepted this arrangement. Today, the Center is known to be equipped with modern medical equipment, and renders excellent service.

Gladstone and Indian pastors also labored in the construction work from time to time. They worked in a manner that pleased the Bishop. In the course of time that Institute developed into a Bible College that prepared pastors needed for the Church in Andhra.

Mrs. Anbu Azariah conducted classes for the wives of the pastoral students. This way, she helped every one of them to [illegible] at least support [illegible] her husband in his ministry.

[illegible]

CHAPTER 6

AZARIAH, THE SPIRITUAL FATHER

"You will save those who hear your doctrine."
I Timothy 4: 16.

Like the rushing of doves to their latticed windows, the number of people rushing to take refuge in the Church kept multiplying all over the diocese. In 1923, within the kingdom of the Nizam of Hyderabad, there were 102,000 Christians. Within the confines of the Dornakal diocese in this kingdom, during the period from 1920 to January 1923, 20,000 people had joined the Christian church.[1] Including this figure, there were 75,000 Christians spread across the Dornakal Diocese both within the Nizam kingdom and outside it. By the end of 1926, there were 150,000 Christians. "The fruit of my ministry is the Mass Movement among the untouchables in villages," said Azariah. "This is the cause for the upswing in the number of Christians. This movement focuses on the socio-economic and religious aspects. But do not think that these people joined the Church in anticipation of receiving 'bread and fish'. The Church offers no worldly benefit. On the contrary, it is these people, whose daily wage is just six paisa, who support the Church with their meager income. Being ordinary farm laborers and leather craftsmen, it is these poor people who have contributed Rs.78,000 last year for the services of the Diocese. The village church ministry is being

1. Figures given by Bishop Azariah at a meeting in Melbourne, Australia, 1923.

done entirely by Indian pastors. The white missionaries have confined their ministries to schools, colleges and training institutes. There are several bodies such as the Diocesan synod, the Bishops' Council, Circles, village Circles, and Church Councils that ensure the democratic functioning of the Church. All these organizations are kept under the supervision of Indians."[2]

"Eighty five percent of the untouchable caste people are illiterate," said Azariah as he attributed his methods of evangelism as the reason for multitudes joining the Church. "Their illiteracy was a problem. It was not possible to educate multitudes of Christians embracing Christianity, whose numbers were rising rapidly, to form a 'church with educated people as its members'. The proclamation of the gospel is now being done through 'the medium of songs'. It is a method akin to wandering Hindu minstrels singing and explaining their scriptures to the accompaniment of music. The Telugu language spoken in our region is reported to be a sweet, melodious language. It is referred to as the Italian language of India. This method is easily practiced in Telugu. People belonging to the untouchable castes are endowed with singing talent. They could sing well from their childhood.

"Rev. Subbiah, a pastor in the Diocese, is an expert in proclaiming the gospel through music to people not yet evangelized," says Azariah after having explained the method of proclaiming the gospel through songs and music. "He has written many Christian lyrics; he has started writing religious dramas too. We have enacted his dramas such as 'Amos' and 'Jeremiah' in many places. Its benefits are many. In a very simple way, people easily knew about Amos and Jeremiah. Subbiah is now writing a drama script on the life of Saint Paul. This method is now spreading to other missions."[3]

---

2. From an address given in England in April 1927: reported by 'the Observer', dated 25th April 1927.
3. ibid

It is fair to expect that the Hindu community would be annoyed with and be jealous of multitudes of Hindus joining the Church by the intensive spread of the gospel through these methods. But, in reality, such reactions were not widespread. Bishop Azariah wondered why the Hindus did not react adversely. Once a high-ranking government officer was asked what he thought about the Christian mass movement. "These multitudes of Christians have learned to live with sober mind, righteousness, justice and fear of God," he replied.[4] Do we need to say that the Bishop's joy on hearing this testimony welled up in thanksgiving and praises to the Lord?

"From the time our farm laborers became Christians, they have been transformed into people of good behavior and utmost integrity in their work," said an upper-caste of the local Hindu communiy to the Bishop when he was visiting a village. "Sir, we are grateful to you for teaching them Christian religion."[5]

One day in 1926, Azariah visited a village to conduct Confirmation Service. A man, who had received Confirmation from the Bishop two years earlier, met the Bishop with the Pastor's help, and greeted the Bishop.

Bishop: "What is the purpose of your meeting me?"

The man: "Two years ago I received Confirmation from you. About 100 to 150 persons received Confirmation from you at the same time. You may not know me."

Bishop: "What's the matter?"

The man: "I would like to narrate to you about how that Confirmation Service proved to be a service when I truly received the Holy Spirit. I was baptized four years ago. But my way of life did not change. I was a drunkard and a thief. I

4. The Record' dated 4th May 1927 reporting the Bishop's address at the CMS Albert Hall meeting, 1927.

5. ibid

cannot tell you what evil I have not committed because I have committed all kinds of evil. On the day of confirmation, I knelt down before the church. After receiving the confirmation, I returned to my seat. 'Lord, you love me,' I said as I prayed to God kneeling down. 'You sent Jesus Christ to die for us. In addition, I have received from you the blessed gift of the Holy Spirit. I shall no longer live the way I lived until now. Grant me the strength to be a new man.'

"After this, I returned home," he continued, as the Bishop listened to him attentively and with concern. "I desired to drink. I was tempted to rob, to return to my old way of living. But I was firm not to yield. My landlord is the wealthiest man in this region. It seems he had been watching me. But he did not enquire from me.

"Because the wages he had been paying me were not sufficient, I requested him to relieve me from my job. 'Alright, you have been serving me the past five or six years,' he said. 'I have been paying you five rupees from the beginning until today. You were satisfied with what I paid you. Why do you suddenly say that your wages are not sufficient?'"

The Bishop raised his eye brows wondering what he was going to say.

"I had to confess to my landlord that I unlawfully earned more than the wages he paid me. 'Did you think that your wages were sufficient unto all of us? No! We had other means of multiplying our income.'

"'But, I cannot do so now. I have surrendered my life to Jesus Christ. Therefore, I cannot live the way I lived earlier. This is why I told you that my wages are insufficient'. My master looked intently at me, and with rapt attention. 'Alright, you wait for a month,' he replied."

The Bishop also looked at that man intently. Many kinds of thoughts and emotions ran through his mind: wonder, joy, longing to know the conclusion of the story. His eyes looked at him tenderly. His heart was excited.

"A month later, the landlord met me. 'I am appointing you as Manager over all the workers,' he said. 'I am also doubling your wages. But do not leave my service. I need you.'"

"Father, what this man Joseph says is all true," said the Pastor who was attentively listening to all what Joseph spoke. "A few days ago, his landlord met me. 'In the past two years, not once have I visited my farm,' he said. 'This man Joseph manages everything at the farm. I trust him completely.'"

"This is just one among many true stories," said the Bishop after narrating the story of Joseph at a meeting. "When I tour my diocesan region, I keep witnessing the great works of Christ and His Holy Spirit in lifting these poor people from their despicable, sin-laden and helpless living, and adorning them with beautiful, holy living. I fall prostrate before the Lord and thank and praise Him."[6]

"Hindu religion is based on caste divisions," wrote Azariah in International Missionary Review. "People of one caste must be kept aloof from people of another caste. This is the scheme of life in Hindu society. Any type of new ideas may attack it, but Hindu religion has the capacity and power to very easily absorb these as long as these do not affect the Hindu scheme of life. It would merge with competing religions. But, what is the Christian religion? It is said that Christ Himself is the Christian religion. It is absolutely true. Nevertheless, it is a way of life. Christian religion is like a family or brotherhood, a social scheme of life, Christ being its center, diameter and circumference. So, there is no

6. Bishop Azariah at the Queen's Hall Meeting – the 128th Anniversary of the CMS London – The Record, 14th May, 1927.

individuality in Christianity. In it, "there is neither Greek nor Jew, circumcised nor uncircumcised, Gentile nor foreigner, slave nor free, but Christ is all and in all." (Colossians 3: 11). The chief end of Hindu religion is an individual person uniting with god. Christian religion lays stress on selfless service to humanity."[7]

In his sermons to the low-caste Christians, the Bishop emphasized again and again that they should proclaim the gospel to upper-caste people, not only through their reformed conduct and selfless service, but also through their words. It appeared that they were reformed in their lives, but were afraid to proclaim the gospel in word. The Bishop's teaching was not futile. After 1920, both in the regions of the Indian Missions and in the regions of other missions, low-caste Christians met in large numbers to do their ministry work. They also distributed gospel tracts. As a result, among people known as Upper-Caste, and among the low-caste people, and among people of the intervening castes, a 'movement' started, which during 1925-26, in a small scale, turned into a 'mass movement'.

In 1924, Bishop Azariah conducted a baptism service in Khammamedu village, where 326 persons were baptized and added to the Church. Out of them 301 persons belonged to the lower castes and 25 persons belonged to the middle castes. Three years later, in the same place, he baptized 117 persons. He was happy to know that a hundred of them were from the middle castes.

Two weeks later, he conducted Confirmation Service in a village that was over forty miles away. One of those who received confirmation also desire to join Christ. The Church has received all of them as

7. Azariah in International Missionary Review – 1928, pages 155 ff. The Bishop often emphasized this truth in his sermons to new and old Christians and in his dialogues with educated Hindu brethren.

ones being prepared to join the church. They have received the Church's teachings. They are now ready to be received in the Church. They requested me to inform you about this matter."*

All over Andhra, people began to honor the Christian religion. Christian teaching became something desirable. Upper-caste people from all these villages began to beg Bishop Azariah to visit their homes. They began to honor church pastors who belonged to low-caste 'untouchable' community, and treat them respectfully, even permitting them to visit their homes. When the local pastors accompanied the Bishop to their homes, they offered them all chairs to sit, while they themselves sat down on the floor as they eagerly listened to Christian teaching. "This is a new attitude," says Azariah. "This new attitude is the good result of works done by God among the low-caste people of Andhra."[8]

During the last century, some Baptist and Anglican missionaries attempted to bring people from upper castes such as Reddy and Brahmin communities to faith in Christ. Higher education centers like the Noble College were established with this in view. They succeeded, though it was in an insignificant measure. But they stopped there! They did not proceed further. Contrary to this, the Christian Church met with success as they sought those who were ostracized. Despite being 'a church of the downtrodden people', it took root in Andhra, and grew, and began to attract even the upper caste people. The administrative history of 'the Missionary Bishop' Azariah bears testimony to this truth.

Earlier, we observed that it was a hard task to find ministers, train them, and ordain them in churches because the Church had now grown large. "Please come forward and help us that we may train workers needed for the growing Indian Church," said the Bishop whenever he visited countries like England, Ireland, Australia, New Zealand and America, placing this

8. ibid

request before those ancient churches. That request did not fall flat. To a large extent Azariah succeeded in using the resources that he received to train ministers of various types, ordain them in churches, and care for their needs. As a result of his good efforts, by 1925 he was able to ordain 90 trained ministers in the Telugu-speaking Anglican churches in Andhra.

The first task that these pastors and the hundreds of pastors who came after them accomplished was to teach the Christian truths to 10, 000 people each annually, thus preparing them to join the Church. They acquainted the newcomers in Christian virtues and values, and prepared them for baptism. This was their first and foremost duty. The catechists assisted the pastors in an excellent manner so that the pastors could do this continually. The second sacred service of the pastors was to prepare the baptized Christians for confirmation.

Apart from these, they had to be on the move performing essential duties like gospel work, work related to sacraments, children's ministry, and shepherding the church.

Bishop Azariah gave top priority to the basics of Christian life such as Bible-reading, meditation, prayer and gospel work. He gave the second place to the Sacraments, particularly Holy Communion, and he gave the third place to Worship services in the Church. In his personal life, he had a special place for three things: the Bible, gospel ministry, and the Holy Communion. Therefore, he had ordered that the pastors should perform their duty of preparing people for Confirmation attentively and diligently. He was quite strict in examining persons who stood before him for Confirmation because of the high regard he gave to Holy Communion.

Regardless of their age, whether young or old, persons coming to him for Confirmation, if they lacked the true knowledge that they ought to have or lacked awareness of their Christian duties, Azariah did not give them Confirmation.

Those downtrodden, poor Christians had been suffering for ages in ignorance and feelings of slavery. To prepare such people for Confirmation is not an easy task. So, the pastors worked hard to prepare them for Confirmation. Nevertheless, they became anxious as the day of the Bishop's arrival drew near. They were afraid of what would happen.

One day, the Bishop came to know that some persons who could not give up alcoholism had turned up for Confirmation. He canceled the Confirmation service on that day.

Sometimes, he would engage in small talk with the poor people thinking that this may drive out the fear they may have before him. "Which is your native place?" he asked a man. But the man replied by giving his name. We may guess how troubled the pastor was, who had painstakingly prepared the man for Confirmation. The Bishop put the same question to the next man. "I am a member of the body of Christ in baptism, and a child of God," he replied, and continued talking. "They gave me this new name," he said at last. The confusion in the pastor's heart was reflected in his face. "What is your native village?" the Bishop asked the third man. He quickly narrated what he had been coached to say. "They vowed three things in my name," he said. The pastor was in tears. The Bishop was stunned. The Confirmation service was canceled that day!

On another occasion, in 1918, they had to travel from Barlabad to Muthiyalubad, a distance of about ten miles. He started with his workers in the afternoon. They reached a hamlet at 7:00 p.m., where they were served dinner. Around 8:00 p.m., they started, but it started to rain. But they continued their journey thinking that they could cover the remaining distance of four miles before the rains became heavy. The soil was black and slushy. The path was muddy and miry. It was dark. It rained heavily. The sound of heavy rains was deafening. The oxen driving the ox-cart were struggling to move forward in the slush. The cart driver struggled to keep the oxen moving.

The cartage moved forward slowly. It was an hour and a half past midnight. Far away was a faint light. Thinking that this may be a village, they turned the cart towards the light. All they had to face was another one hour and a half of struggle. They reached the periphery of the village. The Bishop ordered the workers to go and find out the name of the village.

The workers came with the shocking news that after all the night's trouble they had covered just three miles! They had to travel another seven miles. After six hours, they reached their destination. The rains stopped. They had to travel another quarter of a furlong only. The Bishop's ox-cart went in the front, and the luggage cart followed behind. Azariah had just dozed off, when he heard a loud noise. He jumped off the cart to see what had happened. The luggage cart had toppled. The cook's face was bleeding, even as he was whining. The other three servants were also injured. Although the time was now about six in the morning, it was still dark. The Bishop lit the hurricane lamp and looked for his tincture iodine. He administered first-aid to the injured workers. The luggage cart was reset, and the journey continued. At last they reached their village. No sooner than they set foot in the village, it started raining. It rained the whole day.

The Bishop started his preparations for the Confirmation at the appointed time. Although he had been told that 35 persons were ready for the confirmation, only twelve of them turned up. "Where are the other 23 persons?" asked the Bishop before he started examining them. "Father, only fifteen persons reached here," replied the pastor. "No sooner than she reached here, one woman got her labor pains, and she gave birth to a girl baby. Another woman is about to give birth to a baby. The third woman is suffering from fever." The Bishop laughed.

He began to examine one by one the twelve who came for Confirmation. "Have you been baptized?" he asked the first one. "Father, I do not know," replied the man. His reply shocked the Bishop. "Have you been baptized?" he asked the second man. "I don't remember," the second man replied. There were signs of disappointment on the Bishop's face. "Have you been baptized?" asked the Bishop again. "Father, what do I know?" the third man replied. The Bishop's eyes were weary by now. "Have you been baptized?" he asked again. "Father I truly do not know," the fourth man replied with a heavy stress in his voice. The fifth one was a woman. Her face was bright. The Bishop thought that he could ask her a little tough question. "What was the price our Lord had to pay to redeem human beings?" asked the Bishop. "Father, three rupees," she said without a doubt. The Bishop's face did not betray his feelings, whether he would laugh or cry. He looked at the next woman. She wore a sarcastic smile on her face. Did her sarcasm come from the thought that the previous woman had answered wrongly? Couldn't she answer such a simple question? Assuming that the woman had such thoughts, the Bishop concluded that this woman may have the right answer. "Four rupees, Father!" she replied loudly and enthusiastically to the Bishop's question. And she burst out in a triumphant laughter.

Poor bishop! He was disappointed, but he was not angry. He showed no sign of irritation or sorrow. He decided that only five out of the twelve were qualified to receive Confirmation; so, he gave the five persons Confirmation. The pastor, five catechists and a missionary were present at the Confirmation service. The service was over in 25 minutes. "In all the Confirmation services that I have conducted, this was the briefest one," said the Bishop.[9]

It is a hard task to teach Christian truths to the downtrodden people, whose intelligence level was basic, and help them understand the truths. It was, therefore, no wonder then that the ministers achieved no great success in it. Being aware of

9. The Bishop's letter to his daughter Miss Mercy Azariah, dated August 19, 1918.

this, Azariah did not get angry. But, whenever he observed severe negligence or lack of interest among the ministers – whether they were pastors or European missionaries – he used sharp words to chide them. For this reason, the ministers – both high and low – feared him. Even foreign missionaries trembled at his presence when they visited him. The Bishop, who knew this, began his dialogue with them in a courteous, amicable manner so as to remove their fear. Then, he sent them away happily after he had fulfilled the purpose for which they visited him.

He was strict with his diocesan ministers, and, at the same time, he showed them his deep, heart-moving love. As a result, such confusions as those that happened in the Confirmation service described above did not happen again. "God is the root cause for the growth," said the Bishop when he spoke about the excellent growth of his diocese. "Nevertheless, among man's contributions to this growth, the pastors' contributions stand out. An important cause for the growth of the churches is our Indian pastors who accepted great responsibilities, and worked enthusiastically. Many of them are trustworthy and capable of effectively fulfilling responsibilities that they accepted. By offering the responsibility to Indians, which until now was accepted by English missionaries, there has been no shortcoming."[10] He was able to speak in this manner because of his love and strictness.

In the beginning, Dornakal diocese was confined to a small area within the taluk (sub-division) of Manukot in the Southeastern part of the Nizam's kingdom, and the taluk (sub-division) of Khammamedu. The CMS was engaged in missionary work in Khammamedu region, while IMS operated in Manukot region. In many ways, both these missionary societies worked in co-operation with each other. For example,

10. A Charge to the Clergy, 1920 – quoted by G. V. Job in his 'Samuel Vedhanayagam Azariah.'

students from IMS School in Dornakal were admitted into higher classes at the CMS School in Khammamedu. Students from Khammamedu CMS School were admitted in IMS Crafts Factory. CMS operated in the coastal districts of Andhra known as 'North Circar'. These districts came under British rule and were joined with 'Chennai Rajdhani'. Anglican churches in this region belonged to the Chennai Diocese. The Telugu districts of Kadappa, Kurnool, Chitoor, Bellary and Anantapur were under the British rule and in the Diocese of the Chennai Bishop. SPG Society ministered in these areas. People in the coastal districts, known as the 'Ceded Districts', spoke Telugu as people in the Nizam kingdom did. In his capacity as Assistant Bishop to the Bishop in Chennai, Azariah also served as Bishop of Anglican churches in the Telugu-speaking Andhra districts of 'North Circar' and 'the Ceded Districts'.

In the beginning of his ministry as Bishop, the missionaries and church leaders of these districts were not willing to accept Azariah because he was an Indian. When he visited pastorates like Machilipatnam and Vijayawada to perform his duties, the local people protested by showing him 'black flags'. Azariah ignored these protests as if nothing happened.

Many European missionaries did not like Bishop Azariah visiting their mission fields in his capacity as Assistant Bishop, nor did they like him perform spiritual services. They complained to Bishop Whitehead. But Whitehead ignored their complaints. Some missionaries even sought transfer from areas where Azariah may possibly minister, to other areas. Whitehead ignored their pleas too.

However, in course of time, the church leaders who opposed Azariah by various ways including showing him black flags, in protest, began to plead with Whitehead to post them in Dornakal Diocese under Azariah's authority and loving service. Even he could not believe it. But when he believed it, he rejoiced over it.

On January 8, 1913, Dornakal Diocese was formed with 8,000 Christians and six Indian pastors[11] As a result of Bishop Azariah's governance, guidance, inspiration, motivation and intensive gospel ministry, by 1916 the Diocese had 16,000 Christians and twelve Indian pastors. It is no wonder then that people who noticed this phenomenal growth wanted to come under his governance.

One morning in 1917, Metropolitan of Kolkata, along with Bishop Whitehead, Bishop in Chennai, met with the churches of Andhra Mission. CMS missionaries and pastors met them in Eluru, while SPG missionaries and pastors met them in Nandyal, in conference. They requested that all Anglican missions and churches operating in the Andhra region be brought under the supervision of Bishop Azariah. We need not say that both the bishops happily welcomed this request. Later, when the Bishops' Council met, these two bishops narrated this matter that was discussed at the conference in Eluru and Nandyal. The Bishops' Council authorized the Bishop in Chennai to bring all areas in Andhra within the service and authority of Azariah as Assistant Bishop, which until then had not been brought in. They also requested Azariah to prepare a plan to extend the Dornakal Diocese and make it larger by bringing within its ambit all the Anglican Mission churches. Azariah prepared the plan very wisely with the help of the Spirit of God, and in 1922 presented his plan to the Bishops Council. The Council accepted his plan to extend the Dornakal Diocese to include all of Andhra region. Accordingly, Bishop Whitehead handed over all the Anglican missions and churches in the Andhra region to Bishop Azariah. In 1922, the number of Christians in the extended Dornakal Diocese was about 100,000, while in 1930 (that is, after eight years), with the help of the Mass Movements, it rose to 158,000. In

11. The six Telugu pastors were Bagolu Yohan, Bandaru Satyanatham, Kalangi Yohan, Kalangi Samuel, Sadhanala Alexander and M. Gnanaprakasam. They belonged to the Khammamedu CMS Mission.

1939 (after yet another eight years), the number rose further to 220,000. By 1938, there were 150 pastors.

In 1944, which was the Bishop's last year of service, the number of Christians rose to over 240,000. There were 2,152 churches, 167 Indian pastors, and 1,874 other ministers. There were 34,170 children studying education institutions and Adult Education centers. The Bishop provided facilities for the education of about 50,000 illiterate adults. By 1944, the annual income from Church offerings and other means amounted to about Rs.180,000. About 200 students were being trained at their Teacher Training Institute. The number of patients who were treated at their medical centers was 34,894. The Printing Press, the Crafts Training Center, the Boarding School and other institutions were running efficiently.[12]

CHAPTER 7

AZARIAH, THE ARCHITECT OF CHURCH UNITY

"I ask that they may all be one… in us." John 17: 20-21.

The Church grew and multiplied in the Dornakal Diocese. The Bishop formed in it an administrative structure in order to run it efficiently. As mentioned earlier, he had sub-divided the Diocese into Pastorates and Circles or Areas. As a result, the difference that existed between the CMS Church and the SPG Church disappeared to some extent. He removed the authorities that had been vested in European missionaries and vested them in the Circle / Area pastors. Accordingly, church administration came within the control of Indians. The missionaries did not regret that they were deprived of their authority. They were well aware of the Bishop's wisdom and efficiency; even if they might have regretted it, they did not reveal it.

From the early stages of his life, Azariah held the principle that 'the Church needed freedom'. In this biography, we have observed that this principle flashed brightly here and there. "In India, Indians must administer their own matters, and not foreigners," said Azariah when he laid down his principle. "Be it missionary societies or gospel ministry or church administration or raising a church building or whatever it is, it should be with Indian money, under Indian supervision, using Indian servants and Indian method. It should not be foreign money or foreign power."

We already saw that the Bishop adopted this principle in the running of Missionary Societies (IMS, NMS), and, later, in the administrative setup of his Diocese. He continued to adopt this principle in Christian worship and in the construction of the church.

Western architecture did not allure him. Even the beautiful Meignanapuram church building did not attract him. Kolkata's grand St. Paul's Cathedral did not captivate him. The Bishop was firm in his determination to get the Dornakal Cathedral building built with Indian architectural features, and with Indian money. In structure, he had tall compound walls raised around the church, leaving a wide area between the church building and the compound walls, and a pillared structure at the entrance, which was open on all sides, features that simulate South Indian Hindu temple architecture. At either ends of the church's façade he had minarets raised to resemble a mosque. Inside the church building, the capitals of the pillars were sculpted with images of banana trees, lotus flowers, and the cross, resembling Dravidian architecture. In totality, as far as possible, he introduced aspects of Indian art and culture. In this way, the Dornakal Cathedral differed from other church buildings in India.

Indian cultural practices were incorporated in the church worship services too. All who attended the church had to sit on the floor. Worship songs were all native hymns in Telugu language. He did not like Telugu songs sung to Anglicized or Germanic tunes. This does not mean that he hated Western hymns or music. He played western hymns on his violin, and sang them at home.

Before every church service, he made suitable preparations. He had given pastors clear, firm instructions on this. Anyone conducting church service or preaching sermon without prior preparation would incur his wrath. He would think ahead of the smallest detail. For example, he noted down what stanza would be sung at which place during the first procession into the church before the worship service began. He also noted down what line of which stanza would be sung when they reached the Holy Communion table. His rule was that all things must be done in a proper manner and in an orderly way during the worship service.

He disliked the way offerings were collected. He disliked stretching out the Collection bags as the congregation stood to sing the Offering hymn. He disliked the practice of people dropping a small coin or a rupee note into the offering bag indifferently, without realizing that we 'are offering our tithes and offerings to the Lord out of gratitude'; so, our thoughts should not be roaming somewhere else, not even enjoying the offertory song being sung. "Tithes and gifts are 'not collected, but offered'," he said. He made arrangements for small pots or urns made of metals like copper to be placed in convenient places inside the church. The congregation put their gifts and offerings into these vessels when they come into the church. During the time of the offertory, ushers would take the vessels to the chancel and hand it over to the pastor. During this time, the congregation would be silent, praying within their hearts, asking God to accept their offerings. They should not be singing at this time.

He was fond of introducing Indian culture, traditions and such things in the worship methods. He took some efforts to implement his ideas. For example, in wedding ceremonies, he took some customs and practices from South Indian Hindu marriages, which he considered as good, and applied them in Christian weddings. He gave a Christian flavor and explanation for these. In a Hindu wedding, the bridegroom and his bride would go three times in a clockwise direction around a small fire lit before the priest on the floor. The Bishop made the Christian bridegroom and his bride go around the cross three times in a clockwise direction. He invited the church elders to bless 'the wedding chain' before he blessed it on the sacred table. Before the final benediction, he would tie a corner end of the bride's 'saree' (an unstitched drape about six meters long and a meter broad worn around the hip down by Indian women) to the corner end of the bridegroom's robe. These are a few new practices he introduced in Christian wedding.

Some of his opponents who opposed Azariah's ordination as Bishop had earlier discredited him as one who was 'soaked in Western culture'; however, in reality, Azariah laid stress on Indian methods, customs and culture. He felt that the Church should not put away Indian culture. Indians should be managing church affairs, and need to have full freedom in it. India does not need the terrible woes of divisions prevalent in Western Christianity. It is by the Hindu religion that India is united as one country from Kashmir to Kanyakumari. The moment Westerners preached Christianity and led people to the Christian faith, they also introduced their divisions, dividing the Church into various divisions and causing many evils. "Is it not shameful and foolish to describe ourselves as members of foreign church such as the Anglican Church, Swedish Lutheran Christians, American Presbyterians, Canadian Baptists, and Welsh Methodists?" asked Azariah. "The reason for such divisions is our assumption that we belong to that foreign church which was related to the Mission of that foreign country because that Mission had proclaimed the gospel to us, right in our native place, wherever we were born in this country. It is not our fault that we are divided. Owing to historical situations, the Western Christians are divided among themselves, which is a matter for their concern. There is no meaning in dividing ourselves because they are divided. Moreover, Indian Christians are a tiny minority, and we live in a land among vast multitudes of people of another faith. It is clear that being so few in number, and yet divided into various divisions, is going to harm us, whichever way you see it. We preach one God, one Christ and one Church, but we display many churches as if we believe in many gods and have many Christs! Therefore, we all need to spurn and dismiss the Church divisions that we 'imported from Westerners', and unite as one Indian Church."

Azariah spread these ideas, if possible, whenever he spoke and wherever he spoke, in India and abroad. All Christ churches around the globe should join together as one Church. "The Church's unification may not be feasible in other parts of the world; but, in India, it is an indispensable need," said Azariah very emphatically wherever he went. "Western churches may think that 'the Church's unification is good; but, it is not an indispensable need'. For us Indians, it is our very lifeblood. We have no place here unless we unite."

There were many others in Indian churches who had the same ideas. One of them was Pastor Santiago, leader of the South Indian United Church. Azariah and Santiago sent written invitations to many church leaders in South India (Andhra, Karnataka, Kerala and Tamilnadu) requesting them to attend a meeting in Tharangampadi (Tranquebar), where there will be no European missionaries, and where they would pray for the unity of the Church among themselves and have clear discussions. The invitation was to meet in Tharangambadi (Tranquebar) to pray for and discuss about the Church's unification.

On May 1 and 2, 1919, thirty three pastors met in Tharangambadi. Except George Sherwood Eddy and Herbert Arthur Popley, all the others were Indians. Twenty six of them belonged to the South Indian United Church. The remaining seven pastors were from the Anglican Church. Bishop Azariah presided over the meeting. Rev. S. G. Madhuram (CMS) and Rev. D. Koilpillai (SPG) from Tirunelveli participated in the meeting. The two-day discussions and debates, which were held in the spirit of brotherhood, ended in stressing the need for unity. Finally, all agreed and signed 'the Tranquebar

Manifesto', which was published. According to it, the Anglican churches in South India and the United Church of South India agreed on four basic doctrines, based on which they could form one Church. It was emphasized that "The Holy Bible, the Apostles Creed, the Nicene Creed, and the two Sacraments of Baptism and the Holy Communion" were the four doctrines they agreed upon to be united as One Church. Some other counsel were also given.

From that day, Azariah began to work tirelessly for the unification of the South Indian Church. He participated in all historically reputed discussions on Church unity. It is impossible to narrate here the history of those discussions. "Had Azariah not been there, there would have been no Church of South India today," said those who knew that history well. He did not let the talks fade. He cleared people's doubts, handled the protests, but did not retreat in the face of failures. Rather, he progressed well. He motivated the Indian leaders. When they became weary, he encouraged them. He drove out their fears about their Mother Church in the West, and obtained for them the co-operation and blessing of their Mother Church. He also guarded the local churches that were coming together to form one Church lest they lose their foreign aid. We can keep writing about the works that he had completed for the Church's unity. However, it does not mean that he did all these by himself. There were many others who helped him in this task. But he was the one who spearheaded the action. Whether it was explaining the policy of the Historic Episcopacy or the Unification of Ministry or the Pledge of Protection, it appeared as if the talks may fail over these complicated matters. There were times when it appeared that all his hard work would be wasted. But for Azariah's wise guidance, 'the Tarangambadi Manifesto' would have remained a distant dream.

The twenty-six year old history came to an end. In three years, the Anglican Church in South India, the South Indian

Unity Church, and the British Methodist Church would be merging. The day of forming the Church of South India by merging these three churches was fast approaching. But, Azariah had reached 'the top of Mount Pisgah'.

The Church of South India was the crown of Azariah's achievements. That Church was the first fruit of the International Christian Unity Movement. The architect of that Movement was the Scholar John Raleigh Mott.

From his early days, it became evident that a day would dawn when opportunity would arise for Azariah to become one of the global Church leaders. From the time he began to serve in the YMCA, Azariah's devotion to God, his thirst for souls, and his love for the Lord attracted the attention of John R. Mott. In 1910, through Mott, Azariah received an invitation to attend the World Missionary Conference at Edinburgh. We have already seen the history of Azariah attaining global fame at Edinburgh. A great scholar was amazed at the beauty and skill of Azariah's English speech given on that day. He commented that Azariah's speech was 'a beautiful specimen of polished English'[1]. We may, therefore, say that his extraordinary skill in the use of the English language drew the British people toward him.

It was in 1920 that Azariah made his second trip to England. 'The Annual Conference of the Worldwide Anglican Church Bishops' was held that year at Lambeth Palace. Azariah attended the Conference as a member. "He appeared as the stability and symbol of the common Church in India," said a participant describing Azariah. The Church's Unity was discussed at the Conference. After the Conference, Azariah visited many places speaking in churches and meetings about the ongoing efforts taken to bring about the unity of the churches in South India. Cambridge University honored

1. Rev. William Gurban in 'Great Thoughts' (1910, page 248) writes: "That address was a beautiful specimen of polished English".

Bishop Azariah by conferring upon him the degree of D. Litt.

Three years later, Azariah visited Australia and New Zealand where he was welcomed by the churches there with great joy. Two missionaries, Ms. Walen and Ms. Cain, had earlier come from Australia and served at the Dornakal Diocese. These missionaries had started a 'Lace-knitting' unit at Dornakal, which gave employment to a thousand people. The Bishop praised the work of these two women. He visited many towns and cities in these two countries, where he spoke about Dornakal Diocese and the ongoing efforts to unite the churches in South India. He sought the friendship and aid of the Australian Church.

In 1927, Azariah visited England again, when he was welcomed with greater respect and enthusiasm than before.

On the 27th of April, he delivered the sermon at the Thanksgiving Service of the 226th Anniversary of the SPG Society at the historically famous Westminster Abbey. The same evening he spoke at a public meeting in Albert Hall, where he spoke elaborately on the SPG's ministry in the Dornakal Diocesan areas, and about the ministries of other missions operating in these areas. Here he received financial aid for his Craftsmanship students.[2] He also spoke about the ongoing efforts of the South Indian Christians to unify their churches. "All over India, people are praying with the desire that they all may be one, and they are working towards it" he said. "They have realized that a united Church alone can win India for Christ. We need the sympathies and aid of our Mother Church in England for many years to come. Was not the universal church one? In the work of bringing peoples of the world to Christ, we can achieve positive results only if we all work in union. The time has come to accept the truth that India can come to the knowledge of the gospel only through the Indian Church. The Church in England should contribute to this work

2. 'The Record', 29th April 1927 – Paper Clipping.

by helping the Indian Church. The missionaries they send to India should be helpers and not governors controlling it. In the future, the Indian Christian administrative structure should be "a Church and not congregations attached to Missions of the Mother Church."[3]

After this, he visited some of the bigger cities in England, and returned to London. The Annual Festival of the CMS Society was held there. On this occasion too, he addressed the large gathering at Albert Hall. "Those who had gathered there listened to his speeches with a keen interest and their hearts were excited."[4]

In those days, during a meeting, the Bishop narrated an incident. Mahatma Gandhi, in his writings, used illustrations from several Bible verses drawn from Lord Christ's Sermon on the Mount. Several times he pointed to the Savior's suffering, death, His sacrifice to redeem humankind and such other incidents. So, non-Christians, particularly Hindus, desired to read the Sermon on the Mount and Christ's life history. Those were the times when the printed Bible was not easily available. On one such day, the daughter of a great king in the Andhra region was getting married. Thousands of guests attended the wedding. Desiring to present his guests a memento, the king was happy to give each of them a booklet containing the Sermon on the Mount, which he specially got printed for this occasion. [The Bishop narrated this incident at the Anniversary meeting of the British Bible Society].

He narrated another incident. Mahatma Gandhi was invited to address a College gathering in Bombay (Mumbai). "What is the topic on which you would like me to speak?" asked Gandhi. "Please speak on the Christians' New Testament," replied the students. Pointing out to this incident, the Bishop requested that there should be no obstruction to the printing of

3. 'Church Times' dated 29th April 1927, clipping.

4. The Record dated 4th May 1927.

thousands of the Holy Bible meant for distribution in India.[5]

The Bishop traveled from England to Switzerland to attend a large Conference in Lausanne. The focus of the Conference was on "International Christian Faith – The Church Organization". Among the bishops who represented India were Dornakal Azariah, Bombay Palmer, Tirunelveli Tubbs and Chennai Waller. Rev. Pasumalai Paninga, Rev. Bellary Sumitra, and Nagercoil Parker were the pastors who attended the Conference. At the Conference in Lausanne, the attention of the delegates turned to the efforts taken to unite the churches in South India. But, it was the time when those efforts had slackened. The important reason for this was the hesitation on the part of the Anglican Church Bishops' Council to accept pastors, who were not under the control of a Bishop, in equal terms with their pastors who were under their Bishop. Leaders like Sumitra were not ready to consent to this attitude of the Anglican Church. As a result, the situation in South India was that the talks were about to end in a deadlock.

In Lausanne, Sumitra and Azariah discussed the matter with an open heart. They sought the counsel of other leaders too. "If we were to continue the unity talks only with Bishop Azariah, then the churches will be easily united," said one of the leaders.[6] This leader thought so because Azariah was not self-opinionated in his approach to problems, but respected the opposite point of view too. As far as the unification of the South India Church was concerned, Lausanne ended in disappointment. But South India Church did not get bogged down in arguments and counter-arguments. It wanted to complete the job, and determined to attain unity. There was none other than Bishop Azariah who spoke movingly, and clarified matters in a way that others gave their consent. "In Europe and America, the goal of church unity is something acceptable only in the books, but not in practice," said Azariah

5. 'The Guardian', 12th May 1927.

6. 'Church of South India' by B. Sundkler, page 158.

to emphasize before the Western churches the need for unity. "But in the Mission provinces, it is indispensable for Church life. In Christian countries, church divisions may be the source of its weakness. But, in non-Christians countries, church division could cause adverse effects."[7] The Bishop returned to India after the Lausanne Conference.

After three years, he visited England again. As in 1920, this time also he went there to attend 'the Lambeth Conference', an international conference of Anglican bishops. There, Bishop Azariah, Bishop Palmer, Bishop Waller and other bishops obtained the approval of the Conference for the 1929 Annual Plan for the unity of the South India Church.

In 1930, on his way back from England, he stopped over at Palestine, to visit many places that had become famous through the life of the Savior.

Again, in 1936, he visited Australia and New Zealand. Crowds gathered to hear his blessed sermons. "The gospel of Lord Christ is for all nations and all communities," he said. "Thousands of people in India are seeking Christ's Church and joining it. A new attraction for the Lord Christ has appeared in people." These are just a summary of his speeches.

In the following year, two International Christian Conferences were held in Britain. The Conference at Edinburgh had as its theme, 'Christian Faith and Church Administration'. The Conference at Oxford had as its theme, 'Christian Life and Service'. Azariah attended both the conferences. In the Oxford conference, he served as a vice-president. Preliminary preparations began for merging these two movements into one World Council of Churches. The Bishop's heart rejoiced about this.

From England he went to USA. It was the occasion of the

---

7. Op. cit. page 159.

150th Anniversary celebration of the American Independence, which was celebrated in a grand manner. "It is the duty of the people of the independent nation of USA to establish freedom and human rights wherever people are suffering and suppressed," said Azariah who took part in these celebrations. This is a summary of his moving speeches.

On his way back to India, he again visited England. On May 10, 1937, he was happy to witness the coronation of King George VI.

On January 8, 1938, the Silver Jubilee celebration of the Dornakal Diocese was celebrated. The building of the church that had started in 1915 had not yet been completed. Azariah had determined to get it built only with donations from Indians. But they did not receive sufficient funds. In December 1938, an International Missionary Conference was scheduled to be held at Madras Christian College campus in Tambaram. Azariah had wanted to get the building of the Cathedral completed before this conference. He had to listen to his friends' request that he should accept foreign donations from Christians abroad. From then on, the building project speeded up.

The Tambaram conference was held in the last week of December. It is no exaggeration to say that the Bishop was in his full glory at this International Missionary Conference which was held in his own country. The theme of the conference was 'the Church's Message to the World'. The conference provided him sufficient opportunity to expressly speak on the need for evangelism and our responsibility towards it, which was the burden of his life. And he used his experience in Dornakal to illustrate what he was saying. Although the Mother Churches were not concerned about the unification of the Church, he pleaded with the representatives of younger churches to support, bless and help the younger churches in their unification move. Moreover, the representatives should do this with the support and headship of the Lord, who Himself is the author of Church unity. "The Church in every nation should move away from being 'Missionary Churches'," said Azariah emphatically. "Only by becoming National Churches in each nation can they grow in self-support and self-governance, and accomplish their evangelistic ministry with dignity and responsibility."[8]

Soon after the conference, Azariah rushed to Dornakal. The construction of the Cathedral was completed. The dedication of the new building was scheduled for January 6, 1939.

The foundation stone for the building had been laid on January 14, 1915, but its construction did not start until 1919. From the beginning, Tirunelveli Christians sent their donations separately for the church building project. Because multitudes of people were continuously joining the Church, the Bishop became too busy to allocate time for the church building project. In 1919, 'the white corn famine' hit the region hard and many people suffered from hunger. In order to provide some of them jobs to sustain them, the church building project resumed. Those who were affected by the famine were given jobs like digging pits for the foundation, and laying the foundation. Again the work stopped. From 1932, Tirunelveli Indian Missionary Society with renewed interest came forward to donate money. With this money and the donations that came from Indian Christians, local missionaries, and the American Reformed Church, the church building project progressed. Azariah had desired to dedicate the Cathedral building during the Silver Jubilee celebration of the Dornakal Diocese in January 1938, but it was not feasible. The church building was ready for dedication only at the end of the year. J. S. Muthiah was its civil engineer and architect. The building was 109 feet long and 35½ feet wide. The verandah around the building was 8½ feet wide. The height

8. Christadoss – op. cit. pages 193-194.

of the towers (including the cross on top) was 67 feet. The construction cost was Rs.74,000. In this, the contribution of the Indian Missionary Society and its supporters was Rs.35,000; the contribution of its missionaries and ministers was Rs.2,000; the contribution of the Dornakal Diocese was Rs.11,000; and, the contribution of the American Reformation Church was over Rs.25,000.

The Cathedral's pulpit was a gift from the Kolkata Diocese. The ornate Bishop's Chair was a gift of the pastors of St. Paul's Cathedral in Kolkata. Many things were received as gifts. The Chennai Diocese gifted the bronze lectern for the reading of the Lessons. The Assam Diocese gifted the Sacred Table for keeping books. The Dioceses of Bombay, Chota Nagpur, Lucknow, Nagpur, Lahore, Rangoon and Nashik gifted ornate chairs for pastors. Colombo donated the lamp-stands to be placed on the Sacred Table. A Nellai Christian living in Lahore donated the crosses on the towers as well as the cross on the Sacred Table. The Tuticorin and Nazareth Circles of the Tirunelveli Diocese donated the window panes in the altar area, the Steps leading to the Altar, and a small table to hold sacred things. Different areas in the Dornakal Diocese and the Mothers Fellowship Society gave several other things.

The dedication ceremony was conducted by the Kolkata Metropolitan Foss Westcott.

On January 6, 1939, at seven in the morning, members of the Dornakal Church gathered at the church in the old campus, and thanked God for the church where they had been worshipping for 25 years and for all the services and ministries that were done there. From there they proceeded to the new campus in a procession led by the Assistant Bishop A. B. Elliot. Bishop Azariah stood at the gate of the new campus to welcome them. Now, with Bishop Azariah leading them, they went in a procession singing the litany, and reached the porch. There stood the Metropolitan and bishops from Chennai, Nagpur, Kolkata (Assistant Bishop), Guildford (England), Ohio (USA), Aotearoa (New Zealand Maori), and Sierra Leone in Africa, along with other eminent persons. After Archdeacon F. F. Gladstone read the handing-over document all of them went around the Cathedral in a procession led by the Metropolitan. When they reached the main entrance door of the Cathedral, Mr. Muthusamy handed over the keys of the door to the Metropolitan. Mr. Muthusamy was an experienced missionary of the Indian Missionary Society. He was the one who worked hard and played a major role in the construction of the Cathedral along with the Civil Engineer and Architect J. S. Muthiah. Having received the keys, the Metropolitan formally opened the main door of the Cathedral. When they entered, the entire congregation inside the Cathedral stood up. Bishop Azariah gave thanks to God in a way that moved people's hearts. After this, the Metropolitan and the other bishops consecrated the Cathedral, its furnishings, vessels, utensils and all the holy things in it. At last, the Metropolitan declared that the Dornakal Cathedral has been consecrated in the name of the Triune God as the glorious Temple of His Presence.

Dornakal Church was the daughter of Tirunelveli Church, and Bishop Azariah its young son who built the world famous Dornakal Cathedral. And it was fitting that the first Divine Service held there was the ordination of Rev. S. C. Neil as Bishop, who was chosen by the Mother Church in Tirunelveli. Azariah's long standing desire to build a Cathedral and dedicate it during his lifetime was at last fulfilled. And it ended very well with the ordination of Rev. Neil. All these events gave him joy and overwhelmed his heart with thanks and praises to his Lord. His heart, filled with deep love for Lord Jesus Christ and rapturous devotion to Him, was simple and elegant which were symbolized in the Cathedral that stood simple and elegant. May that church, which today stands as a testimony to the Lord of Azariah, always stand as a shining testimony.

CHAPTER 8

AZARIAH, THE INDIAN BISHOP

"May his name be famous in Israel."
Ruth 4: 14

The year 1939 brought a turning point in world history. The Second World War began in the closing months of that year. In the West, Hitler's Germany marched triumphantly conquering several lands and subduing, in a few months, a vast portion of Europe. It subdued several countries in Africa one after another, and came close to Egypt.

In India, according to the Law promulgated in 1935, the Congress party ruled in provinces from 1937. The party opposed the move made by the then British government to involve India in the Second World War in favor of the British and against Germany. The British never consulted the Indian people. So, the then Congress government resigned and started the Non-Cooperation Movement. Many of its workers were arrested and put in jail.

The battle was drawing close to India. By the end of 1941, in the East, Japan finally entered the war. It conquered China and those Asian nations that were then ruled by European countries. It subdued Burma (Myanmar) and Malaya (Malaysia), and came so close to India that any moment it would invade India. Mahatma Gandhi and the Congress President agreed that Germany, with its allies Italy and Japan, had started this unjust war, and if they won, it would result in catastrophe for the world. Accordingly, they issued several declarations. At the same time, they believed that India should tell Britain, “We will not help Britain in the war unless they grant independence to India.” They did this believing that this was one way India could attain independence from Britain.

So, leaders were arrested. Immediately, there was a rumbling across the land. Riots broke out in many places. On the one side, there was anxiety that the enemy would cross the border into India any moment. On the other side, there was turmoil within the country.

In this time of crisis, it was natural that the Indian Christians looked up to its one Indian leader for his counsel and guidance. “Christians should not join the riots against the government,” said Azariah, giving counsel that ought to come from a Christian leader. “A Christian has no place in any movement that gets involved in acts such as murder, looting the public, destroying property and burning them, whatever the motive be. What the British government does is unjust indeed. In its struggle for independence, the Congress party opposes this injustice. Nevetheless, ‘any party that desires to bring good by evil means’ will eventually cause evil to the nation. A Christian should have no part in it.”

Azariah became the target of criticism for this attitude as his critics declared him unpatriotic. But history proves that among the Christian leaders of his time, there was none more patriotic than him. Way back in 1910, in several places in England, he spoke in support of Indians’ thirst for independence. He felt that one way to be satisfied is that the 1920 Montague-Chelmsford Reforms would pave the way for India’s independence. In 1927, in several places, he spoke on his ideas about Independent India and Democracy.

Azariah not only described himself as ‘a Christian first, and an Indian next’, but also taught that Indian Christians’ patriotism should come next to and below our love for Christ. He never changed his position on this.

Firmly holding the view that Christ's Church should not consider itself different from the Indian Society, Bishop Azariah strongly opposed the demand for special representation for Indian Christians in the future independent India, which was a matter of discussion during 1932-33. "Indian Christians are Indians," he said. "In no way they are different from other Indians. Moreover, Christianity is beyond all divisions that divide human society. Its aim and service is to eliminate divisions and discords, and not to create them." By stressing these basic values, Azariah brought victory to Indian Christianity in the freedom struggle.

As firm as he was on Indian Church affairs that the Church here belongs to Indians, and should be freed from the control of Westerners for it to grow, so firm was he in his view that the Indian nation cannot grow unless it attains independence. So, he desired that India should attain freedom, and he also spoke about it openly.

Although he worked hard all his life that the South Indian churches should evolve into one single Church, he did not live to see it happen in 1947, just as he longed for India's freedom and looked forward to it, but he never lived to see it happen in 1947. Who will not think of this, and grieve?

Indians were troubled when the Japanese armies came close to our border. It was expected that any moment Japanese fighter jets would bomb the coastal towns of Andhra region. Government authorities had requested the inhabitants of those towns to be ready to evacuate at short notice and save their lives. It was in these panic-stricken days of anxiety that the Bishop traveled to Andhra region to console and solace his people. He spent many days with them. He preached sermons that solaced them. He committed them to the grace and protection of the loving Lord. The people experienced first-hand the love and solace of the Bishop and were consoled.

When orders were issued for them to evacuate their town to save their own lives, most of the Christians in the coastal towns did not evacuate for they had been taught to have strong faith in their God in times of trouble.[1] The Bishop had ordered the Church workers, especially the pastors, to remain with members of their respective churches and support them. Accordingly, they remained with the people and supported them.

If India attains independence, responsibilities would increase. Before attaining independence, it is necessary that the nation progresses in various departments, especially in the Education Department. The Indian government conducted nationwide Census once in ten years and published them. Even during his YMCA days, Azariah used to carefully scrutinize the results and information in the Census to see if there was progress in the previous ten years, and be satisfied or be dissatisfied with them. He noted down his observations of the 1907, 1911, 1921, and 1931 census results by comparing them and studying them.

Although he exulted over the 'service to the nation' rendered by Christian missions and churches in the areas of Education, Health and the Care of Orphans; yet, he felt that these were not enough. He felt that the missions and churches did not render assistance to the extent they ought to have done. He realized that one of the reasons for this situation was that the Missions of the various churches held back their assistance when they were asked ro co-operate with other missions/churches.

Among the many useful ideas that came from the 1910 Edinburgh Conference, the idea to explore ways and means

---

1. Bishop Azariah's Easter Day Sermon at Machilipatnam, 1942.

of co-operating with one another was specially noteworthy.* In 1911, when the 'Follow-up Committee' of the Edinburgh Conference met at Auckland, it requested John R. Mott to communicate to the churches in the East the actions of and the ideas emanating from the Conference. Accordingly, in 1912, he visited Sri Lanka, India, Burma (Myanmar), Malaya (Malaysia), China, Manchuria and Japan, and completed his responsibilities. In December 1912, India's fifth Annual Missionary Conference met in Kolkata. Mott's speech at the Conference led to the formation of Indian National Missionary Council[2] which was an excellent 'Tool for Co-operation'. This Council was later renamed as 'National Christian Council' with Nagpur as its headquarters. We know that it still functions.

From the very inception of this Council Bishop Azariah showed interest in and concern for its services. Many are the efforts taken and constructive actions completed by the Council for advancing the life of Indian Christianity. We cannot describe these here for want of space, but we can only say that in fifty years of the Council's service, fifteen years of work were completed when Bishop Azariah was its President from 1929 to 1944.

Another Indian Christian institution like the National Christian Council was the 'Bible Society of India'. Several branches of 'the British and Foreign Bible Society' were instituted from 1811 at Kolkata, Chennai, Bangalore, Bombay (Mumbai) and other places for the purpose of printing the Holy Bible in several Indian languages, and distributing them. From 1928, Bishop Azariah served for several years as a Vice-President of the British and Foreign Bible Society. When the idea was floated that India should have its own Bible Society, more than anyone else, it was Azariah who evinced great interest in it, and worked intensively to get it started.

In March 1943, all its branch societies in India held a

2. Christadoss – Op. cit. page 153. **Ibid pages 155 - 159.

conference. Bishop Azariah presided over the conference. The Conference passed resolutions to form 'India – Ceylon Bible Society'. Accordingly, in November that year, the Society was established. Azariah presided over the initial General Body meetings of the Society. The meetings were held for three days. The General Body elected Azariah as the first President of the India – Ceylon Bible Society.

When efforts were taken to revise the 19th Century translations of the Tamil Bible and the Telugu Bible, Azariah served as a member of the Translation Revision Committee of the Tamil Bible, and as the President of the Translation Revision Committee of the Telugu Bible.[3]

Although, in this way, Azariah was involved in various Christian institutions, services and ministries, he performed efficiently the administrative duty of his own large Diocese, and traveled abroad several times, and travelled within India wherever he was invited, and rendered necessary help. Above all, he continued his evangelistic work. He served his Savior from five in the morning to midnight. He wrote some valuable books. Some of these are: 'Bunch of Prayer-Meditation'; 'Christian Charity'; 'Christian Marriage'; 'Christian Married Life'; * 'Christianity and India'; 'South Indian Unity'; 'Holy Baptism'; 'The Sabbath Day'. Apart from these, he wrote numerous pamphlets, and innumerable letters. He also wrote Commentaries on the books of the Holy Bible: I Corinthians; II Corinthians; Job; Revelation. He also wrote many Sermons to serve as aids to the church deacons and ministers. The Circular letters that he wrote to his pastors manifest his vast experience in shepherding the Church. They were like Handbooks explaining how to handle hardships, temptations / tests, and weariness. Until today, we know and experience the service rendered by the Tamil Christian periodical 'The Light of the Tamil Church' to Tamil Christians. It was Azariah who

3. J. S. M. Hooper, letter dated 19th February, 1945.

had started this periodical.

It is surprising how Azariah maintained his house-work balance. Although he was immersed in the service of the Church, he paid individual attention and concern in the life of every member of his family. Whether he was busy with the International Church Conferences held in distant places like England, America and New Zealand or busy conducting meetings in large churches abroad, he did not forget, even for a moment, his family matters or his dear wife Anbu or his precious children. Once in two or three days, he wrote letters to them. Many times he wrote personal letters to each of his children. It appeared as if he wrote those letters to develop their knowledge because he described the many places and scenes that he had seen. He added some brief teachings and counsel for their spiritual growth.

The Bishop proved himself to be an upright Christian father by showing more concern for his children's spiritual life rather than their worldly life. To prove this fact, we give some extracts from the letters that he wrote to his children.

"A true Christian's qualities are to trust in God and to walk humbly before man. This will grant him joy and a useful life. Seek the grace of God for His guidance in every step you take in life. Then you will know His will and plan for your life.

"Ask God to grant you incidents and suitable opportunities in line with His will for your life. His will is to grant you abundant spiritual benefits and to provide suitable opportunities for you to do good, as much as you can, to the people of the world. Always this is God's will for His children. If we attempt to lower God's standards for us, we cannot obtain the higher things that He would like to give us.

"The man who knows God and obeys Him, and lives trusting in God, that man would make himself happy and others happy… The man who trusts God would seek His help through prayer. The man, who studies the Holy Bible and learns from it will find God's wise guidance. By worshipping God and having fellowship with God, he will receive the Holy Spirit and strength.

"May God grant you love and humility! It is useless to have everything else, but not have these two qualities. These two qualities can be received by walking in close fellowship with Christ, prayer, Bible-reading, and by having a conscience devoid of offence. Keep a careful watch on your own self. Confess your faults to God. He loves you. He cares for you. He died for you."

We can quote many such words from his letters, but we are short of space. They may not be needed. These are enough.

God's matchless gift to Bishop Azariah in this worldly life was his dear wife Mrs. Anbu. She was a model Christian wife. The bond of love between Azariah and Anbu was peerless. Next to God's unlimited grace, the reason for Azariah's victorious life and his matchless magnificence was none other than Mrs. Anbu. This is sufficient to comprehend the virtues of this upright wife.

What a blessing it is to be the children of Azariah and Anbu! Like the father, the mother too considered the spiritual life of her children of higher value than their physical well-being. It is enough to give one quote from one of her letters to her children to prove this truth.

"My only request to you is that you may live as a child having genuine faith in Lord Jesus Christ, and as a son who does not yield to the dangerous temptations that come along with the modern civilization. Make your parents' heart happy… I desire that you read the Bible daily and meditate, and that you take part in the Holy Communion every Sunday."

The children who filled the Bishop's palace were the eldest child Mercy, the second child Edwin,

George, Grace, Henry and the last son Ambrose. They also had a son named Martin, who died in 1906, as a 52-day old baby. One of the twins born to them in 1909 passed away soon after birth. James, the other twin boy, died a couple of months later. The birth and death of these three children made Mrs. Anbu very weak. "After we had experienced the sweet fellowship of our babies for a season, God has taken them to Himself," wrote Azariah in a letter to his wife. "Through this experience, God is granting us an opportunity to know His love in a greater measure." In all her ways, Mercy was equal to her father. For several years, she was a very present help to her father in his work and administration. She helped him by holding supervisory positions in the Mission institutions in Dornakal and in the Bishop's Secretariat. The Dioceses of Dornakal and Tirunelveli jointly revived the Khondwana Mission that had been started by CMS in Madhya Pradesh, but had been abandoned by it later. Soon, Mercy, with her father's permission, began to work there as a missionary. Edwin passed out from a medical college and became a reputed doctor. George trained to become a pastor, and served as a pastor, first in Tirunelveli Diocese, and, later, in Dornakal Diocese. For many years he served as President of 'the College of Theology' in Dornakal. Azariah's second daughter Grace married Aaron, a Tamil pastor. Another son Henry completed his advanced studies in Agriculture, and worked, first, in Allahabad, and, later, in Katpadi. His next son Ambrose took up a job in the state government, and rose up to high position in the Registration Department. Three of his sons married girls from the families of missionaries of the Indian Missionary Society. Edwin married the daughter of Rev. D. S. David. Henry married the daughter of Canon J. Sreenivasan. Ambrose married the daughter of Rev. Jel Knight. George married the daughter of Moses, a Tahsildar (Revenue Officer), who was Mrs. Anbu Azariah's brother, and an ardent supporter of the Indian Missionary Society.

Bishop Azariah did not show any favoritism to any particular friend or co-worker or any missionary from Tirunelveli. He held that all servants of God are equal. He gave no place for hierarchical classifications such as high or low in God's service. In granting honorary positions at the Diocese, he did not allow excessive authorities to be heaped upon any one person. As far as possible, he did not consent to one person holding more than one post or position. This does not mean that he paid scant respect to the ability or efficiency of the workers. His aim was only to afford several persons an opportunity to work.

He did not work with narrow parochialism when considering reccomendations such as 'He hails from my native place'; 'He belongs to my caste'; 'He is a stranger'; 'He is a foreigner'; and so on. When it was decided to appoint an Assistant Bishop in the fast-growing Dornakal Diocese, he selected Rev. A. B. Elliot, who was his European assistant and President of the Dornakal College of Theology. In 1935, Elliot was ordained as the Assistant Bishop.

"Bishop Azariah had consistently stood for 'Indian Church', 'Indian Supervision', 'Authority in Indian hands', 'preaching the gospel using Indian methods', 'India', and 'Indians'. Could he not elect an Indian as his Assistant Bishop?" It was hard to answer this reasonable question. Some of the charges against him were: "He could not bear to see another Indian becoming a Bishop like him." "He never had confidence on the skills and ability of Indian pastors." "He served as Bishop for 22 years, but did not appoint an Indian as his Assistant Bishop. Nor did he have the foresight to prepare an Indian to succeed him as Bishop." Even today there are some who lay these criticisms against him. Bishop Azariah did not have to pacify anyone who criticized him for selecting Rev. Elliot. Twenty five years ago, in 1909, the Englishman Bishop Whitehead decided that he needed an Indian as his Assistant Bishop, and selected Azariah. "He picked Azariah from among thousands of Indian Christians, although Azariah was still young and a layman who had not been ordained even as an Assistant Pastor," said his critics. "Despite several legal objections, charges of breaking established convention, and objections from missionaries, and several other oppositions, Whitehead selected Azariah. In 1935, after 25 years, in the absence of objections and oppositions, could not Azariah select one from the hundreds of thousands of Indian Christians? Could he not pick one from the 120 ordained pastors in his own Diocese?"

In the same way, except one or two Indian Archdeacons, all the rest were Westerners. After the death of Archdeacon Subbiah, his place was given to Rev. F. F. Gladstone, a European. These actions of Azariah still remain a mystery when seen against the backdrop of Azariah's image as one who strongly favored Indian leadership.

But we can say one thing confidently about Azariah. He always took an action only after ensuring in his heart that it was in accordance with the will of God. He brushed away any criticism. When he believed that what he did was necessary for the development and life of his Diocese, he was willing to set aside even his own ideas and principles, if necessary. "Churches that are 200 years old still believe that only under the leadership of Europeans can their churches' well-being can be sustained," said some experienced Telugu pastors. "They find fault in him that he has selected a European to assist him in the great service of developing hundreds of thousands of common folk in our Church, which had been young forty years ago, while this Diocese is still about 20 years young. Such criticisms as these are meaningless talk, and only reveal the ignorance of these critics." The Telugu pastors' defense of Azariah is certainly worthy of acceptance.

Bishop Elliot was a right hand man to Bishop Azariah. He lived in Khammamedu. He was a bachelor. "He was a saint," said some.[4] Archdeacons gave him their utmost co-operation. "In Azariah's view Canon Gladstone and Elliot were two pages of the same sheet of paper.[5] When Azariah took charge as the Dornakal Bishop, all European missionaries resigned and gave up their jobs. Elliot was the only one who held on to his job.* Elliot was unto Azariah as Joshua was unto Moses, and as Elisha was unto Elijah."*

Archdeacon Subbiah and Pastor Mallelu David were excellent poets and Bible scholars. Bishop Azariah made good use of their talents. * Whenever he discovered persons with excellent skills, Azariah engaged them in the service of the Diocese. If he found anyone short of skills in his work, he did not get angry with him. On the contrary, he counseled him and encouraged him. But if he found anyone lacking honesty and integrity, he warned him. If he still persisted in his old ways of living, he dismissed him. He gave the same treatment to those who spoke lies or rebelled against their higher authorities. "On one occasion, fifteen catechists submitted a written complaint containing charges against a pastor. The Bishop investigated into the allegations. Finally, it was confirmed that all the allegations against the pastor were false. Immediately, he dismissed all the fifteen catechists. Some of them had been working for 30 years as catechists."[6]

The moment he meets a person, Azariah would determine his or her character and skills. "He would determine who is fit to fill which post in which place in his Diocese. His assessment would be 100% correct.** Once he decides to post a person in a particular position, that person should take up that position and go there. If a person refuses to go there, he or she should resign from the service at the Diocese. There was a young missionary with certain talents and skills. One of the missionary

---

4. Interview in March 1974 with Rev. I. B. John, Rev. K. Luke and others.

5. Interview in March 1974 with Rev. I. B. John, Rev. K. Luke and others.*

6. ibid.**

societies had sent him. The Bishop interviewed the candidate. Azariah welcomed him cheerfully and offered him a different job, because he had already appointed another suitable person in the position for which this young missionary had applied. The young missionary disliked the alternative job that Azariah offered. The candidate began to argue that his Mission Society had sent him for a specific job for which Azariah had sought a candidate. "I need a European missionary to fill a specific position in a particular place," said Azariah quite firmly to the candidate. The missionary was adamant that he had come to do what his Mission Society had asked him to do. The Bishop tried to convince him, but it was futile. Finally, he called the Treasurer and told him: "Give the missionary the sum of money that he needs to return to his country."

"You may go," Azariah said to the missionary.

Only after he came out of Azariah's room, the missionary understood his situation. He came in with prejudice looking down on Azariah, the Indian, but what he saw was an Indian Bishop! He ran into the Bishop's room, seeking another interview. Azariah denied it. He pleaded with him for three days to grant him an interview. He tried to influence Azariah with recommendations. Azariah did not relent. On the third day, the missionary left. [7]

Ministry belongs to the Lord. Souls redeemed by His blood are the beneficiaries of a ministry. That being the case, a servant of God should be duty-conscious, enthusiastic, humble, and sincere in his duty.

Azariah showered his great love on those whom he served, especially on village Christians. He visited villages, stayed there, and engaged them in friendly talks. He gave a sympathetic hearing to their woes and problems. He did whatever he could to alleviate their sufferings. He made them happy. He developed their Christian knowledge by teaching

7. ibid.

them truths in the Holy Bible, and by preaching wise sermons and scriptural expositions. It was these work that inspired him and made him happy.

He wished that pastors should serve the way he did, in their own ministries. "Pastors should visit village churches on alternate days, stay there, and do both earthly good and heavenly good to the people," he advised his pastors.[8] Bishop Azariah realized that large missions in Tirunelveli like CMS and SPG were based in Palayamkottai and Nazareth. As a result, other places in their Dioceses, especially the rural areas, did not receive opportunities to develop as the two cities did. So, when he set up public institutions in his Diocese, he set them up in various places.

Some examples of this are given below:

Printing Presses : Dornakal, Machilipatnam.

Leather Tanning Factories: Dornakal, Vidhya Nagar.

Weaving Factories: Dornakal, Gidalur, Vidhya Nagar.

Lace Embroidery Factory : Thummagudem.

Carpentry : Nandhikottur.

He sent blind children to the Lutheran Mission Blind School at Rentachintala, Deaf-and-Dumb children to the Chennai School, lepers to Dichpally, and Tuberculosis patients to Madanapalle. He built a separate treatment center in Dornakal for Leprosy patients. He held Treatment Campaigns for Lepers in the Circle areas.

Azariah also made arrangements for Village Workers to undergo short-term training in Medical science. Dr. William

8. ibid.

helped conduct these training classes. Pastors, catechists and lay-preachers were given a Medical Kit to be kept in their homes. They were asked to give first-aid and simple remedies to poor people in villages. They could replenish the medicines once every six months.[9] The Bishop developed plans to bring physicians and compounders (chemists) on short-stay basis to villages affected by deadly, contagious diseases like cholera.*

Earlier, we had mentioned that one of the many services the Bishop rendered to village Christians was settling them in other plots of land when they were dispossessed of their own plots of land. The alternative plots of land given to them belonged to the Diocese. In a fertile area, there is a village called Garla. In 1919, Mr. A. S. Appasamy of Palayamkottai bought forty acres of land there, and donated it. Bishop Whitehead donated sixty acres of land. A Telugu Christian called Chinta Abraham donated eight acres of land. All these lands were donated to the Indian Missionary Society. The students of Dornakal Teachers Training School cultivated seventy acres of this land.

Meduthapalle: Rev. Samuel Packianathan bought a piece of land and developed a grove.

Once, Bishop Azariah and his assistants traveled by road on the Khammamedu-Warangal Highway. On the way, they stopped by a garden for their meals and a little rest under the shade. A little distance from the garden was a small hillock. Looking at it, he exulted. It would be a good idea to have a small Christian village there, he thought. He planned to have a Boys' Boarding School and a Medical Center there.

Under the Bishop's orders, Rev. K. Luke and Rev. M. P. Israel made enquiries about the land, and bought 150 acres of land. The Bishop named the planned village there as 'Model Village' or 'Madhiripuram' in Telugu. He appointed Rev.

9. ibid.

Canon Sreenivasan as the first missionary to that village. Today, a fine Boarding School is functioning there under the IMS missionary Miss Jayamani. Before her, Miss Koilpillai served there as missionary. It was the Bishop's desire that the Model Village should serve as the center for evangelism ministry.

Azariah did not hesitate to receive help from various quarters for evangelical work in the vast region of his Diocese. In 1922-23, he visited Travancore. His sermons there stirred up the Malayalam congregation there, and in 1924, they volunteered to do missionary work in Dornakal diocesan area. They started mission work keeping Barkal (Karimnagar district) far away in the northern part of the Diocese, as their base station.

"Christians should not think that only outsiders should come and proclaim the gospel, and that is not their responsibility," said Azariah emphatically right from the beginning of his ministry. "It is the duty of every Christian to proclaim the gospel. Before inviting outsiders to preach the gospel, they should start missions and do the work of the ministry." He put it into action by starting the Mulag Mission in 1918 within five years of his ordination as Bishop. This ministry started in Mulag in another part of Warangal district. Missionaries were sent there from Khammamedu circle. Khammamedu and Dornakal circles supported the work financially.

Dornakal Diocese region was noted for the Lambadi tribe. With their strange customs and practices, this tribe hailed from which country? When did they come? Why did they come? How did they come? These are questions for researchers. Some think that they came from Eastern Europe or Central Asia or Germany and settled in the northern part of Italy around A. D. 5, in the Lombardy region. Were they a branch of the Lombard tribe there who somehow migrated to India and settled down in Andhra Pradesh? Whatever their origins, in their religious practices and lifestyle they were different from the Hindus around them, and did not receive the gospel, and for a long time kept themselves apart.

In 1934, the Cholera epidemic struck India, and many died of it. Although Lambadis lived separately in their '*Thanda*', an encampment, and drank the spring waters, many of them died of Cholera. The evangelists who proclaimed the gospel to them also fled. The poor, uncivilized Lambadis were in misery with nobody to help them. Rev. Jel Knight, a missionary of the Indian Missionary Society, volunteered to help them and support them. The physician Dr. William, Jel Knight and some Telugu ministers worked night and day among the tribal people, dispensing medicines and supporting them. Thus they saved many of them from death.

The Lambadis tasted the love of Lord Jesus Christ through these good works of His servants. From then on, hordes of them entered the fortress of salvation. Even today, many Lambadis are still coming to the Lord. All through his life, Bishop Azariah paid special attention to these people, winning their hearts with his love and support, and filling their hearts with love for their loving Savior.

CHAPTER 9

SAMUEL AZARIAH, THE TRIUMPHANT

"Enter into the joy of your Lord." Matthew 25: 2.

It was eight in the morning, and it was a dry wilderness area. The path of the bullock-cart was rugged. The man driving the bullock-cart let the bullocks go at their own pace without goading them because the bullocks had been walking many hours that night. In intervals, he shouted at the bullocks to goad them. A little away from the pathway, some 20 or 30 cattle were grazing. A boy, a herder, was herding them. He wore no clothes except for a foot-long loin cloth like underwear. He held a smoothed stick in his hand. He came running to the bullock-cart. He was thin, and his skin was black. His hair was unkempt. He was about 14 or 15 years old.

He peeped into the cart and stood there gaping. He looked inside with wonder, his eyes open. He whispered something with a lisp. With his hands raised towards the cart, he looks at the man inside the cart. With folded hands, he prostrates before that man. The cart stops. The man driving the cart shouts at the boy, saying, "Get up and give way for the cart." He arose, and directed his folded hands towards the man inside, in an Indian worshipping posture. Walking behind the cart or going around, the boy began to sing and dance.

Bishop Azariah, who was sitting inside the cart, was amused. He sent a catechist sitting with him inside the cart to find out what the boy wants.

"Who are you?" the catechist asked the boy despicably.

"Why are you dancing? What happened to you? Do you need anything?"

The boy is amazed. "What's this?" thought the boy. "Why is he asking so? Is he mad?"

"Are you asking me?" the boy asked. "If human beings see a god, will they not dance and sing?"

"Whom are you referring to?" asked the catechist. "You mean 'the father'? He is a human being. He is just a man like you and me."

""He may be a human being for you," replied the boy in an angry tone. "For me and my people he is a god in flesh. Mind your business and go!"

The 'father', who was listening to their conversation, got down from the cart. "My loving God, all honor and praises belong to you," the Bishop prayed within his heart. "Jesus, show him the Father." The Bishop went close to the boy. The boy began to retreat with his hands still folded. The Bishop embraced the boy. He lowered his natural stentorian voice, and looked at him tenderly. He held the boy by his shoulders, and explained to him the love of the loving God.[1]

Such scenes were part of the Bishop's life. Such were the love and gratitude that the local people had for him. Village launderers have honored him several times by spreading their change of garments before him. When they heard that the Bishop was visiting their village, they would walk miles beyond the village entrance to receive him. Then they would lead him in a procession into their village singing songs.

Were the people of Dornakal the only ones to love him so much? Nay! Wherever he went, people honored him.

1. Heard in Dornakal.

He never forgot the warm welcome the people of his native place Tirunelveli accorded him when he first visited their city after becoming Bishop. At Madurai railway station, at Virudhunagar railway station, and thereafter at every railway station on his route to Tirunelveli, people gathered to welcome him. Members of the Palyamkotai church walked up to Gangaikondan and Thazhaioothu railway stations and there boarded the same train to travel with him to Tirunelveli Junction railway station (former Tirunelveli Bridge railway station) in order to accord him a massive, grand welcome. From there they went in a procession led by the Tirunelveli Bishop to Palayamkotai city, and to 'the Market'. From there they turned South to 'the Fort Shop', crossed the Centenary Hall, and reached the Trinity Church. There they held a Thanksgiving Service.[2] Eyewitnesses to these events still enjoy talking leisurely at length about it.

In 1914, after the death of Bishop A. A. Williams, Bishop Azariah was given additional charge of the Tirunelveli Diocese for a brief period from July 1914 to November 1915. The people of Nellai exulted in this. In those days, whenever he visited Tirunelveli Diocese, in every village he visited, he received grand welcome.

Members of the Tirunelveli Church desired that Azariah should leave Dornakal and become Bishop in Tirunelveli. But there was no indication that Azariah desired it. Only a few years had passed since the time he assumed the position of Dornakal Bishop, and that was the main reason.

From the time that Waller took over as the Tirunelveli Bishop, somehow the idea caught on that he would not be there for long. It was thought that Waller would be transferred to Chennai when the Bishop's post there fell vacant. This made the Church leaders worry that, once again, Tirunelveli would lose the services of a Bishop for a short period.*

2. Letter to Mrs. Azariah, March 1913.

In 1928, when Right Reverend N. H. Tubbs was transferred to Rangoon (present day Yangon), members of the Tirunelveli Church desired that Azariah should be moved to Tirunelveli. Although Azariah liked the idea, he felt it was hard to leave Dornakal. He often mentioned that he loved Tirunelveli and Dornakal alike. After giving a thought to it for a long time, he decided that Dornakal needed his services more than Tirunelveli did. [3]

The last time he visited Tirunelveli was in 1943, when Hindu and Muslim brothers joined Christians to welcome him in Tuticorin. When he saw it, tears welled up in his eyes. "The only reason for this is that I am a slave of Lord Jesus Christ," said he in all humility and gratitude, and ascribed all honor to his loving God alone. "You have honored, not a Bishop, but an evangelist," he told them. "Therefore, you have not honored me, but you have glorified Christ who came to redeem and possess us."

At that time, Azariah was 69 years old. Although he was getting old, he was not getting weak. He was performing his duties industriously and enthusiastically as usual. He displayed the same keenness of observation and intellect, the same strictness, the same firmness, the same tenderness, and the same authoritativeness that he had displayed in his youth and middle ages.

Never was his health badly affected. In his middle age, he once suffered a little from toothache. In 1920, when he visited England, he received proper dental treatment and was cured. In 1927, he suffered from diabetes. In the course of time, that was also cured. He suffered for some months of Rheumatism, but was soon healed. In 1930, because he neglected his sleep, he suffered from nervous weakness and physical debility. On the advice of his physician, he took leave for six months, and took rest and treatment in Chennai, and was healed. When

3. Letter of Mr. J. Anbudaiyan, 1915 & 1928, to Bishop Azaraiah.

he toured his Dornakal Diocesan areas, he always took his cook with him so that he could eat hygienic and healthy food and thus protect himself from digestive diseases. Sometimes, his wife accompanied him on his tours. Every summer, on his furloughs, he stayed in the Nilgiris hills. By the grace of God and his dear wife's loving services, his physical health was protected.

On August 17, 1944, he attained his seventieth year.

Azariah never forgot the advice his mother had given him when he was a little boy. When he was just three days old, a Sadhu (an ascetic) visited his native village Vellalanvilai. The ascetic displayed the number 7 to his mother and left the place. He gave no explanation for his action. Since then, when the number 7 appeared on the dates of the calendar such as 7, 17, 27, or in the seventh month July, or in the years 1887, 1897, and 1907, his mother prayed earnestly on the days, months or years that had 7 in them. She feared that on those days, her son Azariah may suffer some calamity. So, she spent more time in prayers for her son on those days.

After Azariah became an adult, he laughed within himself whenever he thought of it. However excellent she was in her devotion to God, he regretted that she suffered from such superstitions. After hearing the story of number 7, Mrs. Azariah also developed a premonition on the number 7. She also gave place, albeit a little, to the fear of number 7 that had gripped her mother-in-law.[4]

On his 70th birthday, Azariah received many birthday greetings from within his Diocese as well as from outside. Among them, the birthday wishes that he received from church leaders in India showed how much they recognized Azariah's rise.

4. Heard in Dornakal.

"May God grant you many more useful and joy-filled years, devoid of sorrow and misery!" said Bishop Halley from Chennai. "Your life and service have inspired and enthused many young people," said National Missionary Society. "Indian Christianity needs your service, as its matchless leader, for many years to come," said Andhra Lutheran Church.

"I am alive today by the grace of God," wrote Azariah in his general letter to all his children. "May the awareness grip us and our children (his grandchildren) that we are fully dependant on the grace of God! If we are wholeheartedly conscious that we are fully dependant on God's mercy, that consciousness will be the freedom granted to us and our children for many generations."[5]

The Bishop and his dear wife spent the whole day with these thoughts and praised God with a grateful heart.

In those days, there was a burden pressing on his heart. "Devotion to God and faith in God that blazed in the early days of the Diocesan churches now seem to be fading away," thought Azariah. "The warmth of love has become cold. Love for the world was increasing." He was not ignorant of the reason for this situation. "To the younger generation, Christ and Christianity had become old for they had heard it again and again," reasoned Azariah within himself. "Christ was fresh unto the previous generation; Christ was beautiful. Compared with their old gods and goddesses, Christ's holiness and divine love melted their hearts. They realized well the difference between their earlier religious experience and their later experience of peace of salvation, and they exulted in the latter. The second generation knew neither the former experience nor the latter experience." Only a man standing under the scorching sun knows the value of the shade. "Christ should be known to the second generation as someone new and beautiful," said Azariah, as he laid this problem before

5. Circular letter to his Children on the Occasion of his 70th Birthday.

his pastors. The problem agonized him in his old age. He motivated them to aptly know their responsibility for this great duty towards the younger generation, and act accordingly.

In the late half of his 70th year, his senility began to show its weakness. Could his worry over the above-mentioned problem hastened his ageing process?

Nevertheless, he accepted invitations from the Marthoma Church and the Anglican Church to conduct a few spiritual meetings in Travancore, and he traveled to Travancore. Although Azariah was a true Anglican, he never hesitated to respect other churches and to commend their development. Therefore, he desired more than anyone else the Church's unity. One of the things he liked was to establish full fellowship with the Marthoma Church. It gave him great joy to see Anglican pastors and Marthoma pastors together participating in the Holy Communion during the meetings in Tiruvalla, Kerala. He remarked this in his last letter published in the Dornakal Diocese magazine.[6]

A few days after he returned from Travancore, he and his wife visited Barkal Mission churches. The seventy-year old Bishop traveled seventy miles by bus. The road was rugged. They were shaken by jolts. And the journey made them weary.

People who came from the Barkal Mission villages warmly welcomed them. He stayed with those poor people and conducted the Confirmation Services there. He exulted in holding conversation with those simple, naïve people, and in teaching them from the scriptures. He visited village after village. He spent the Christmas day 1944 with them. On the 27th, he traveled from one village to another village by bullock cart. On the way, suddenly the bullocks got unruly. Immediately, the Bishop got down from the cart. He escaped without harm. Did he actually escape without harm?

6. Dornakal Diocese Magazine, January 1945, pages 4 and 7.

On the 28th, he reached Dornakal. He was tired and weary. His body ached. As soon as he reached his house, he went to his room. He fell on his bed with his boots on. The next day, his body temperature seemed to have shot up as he was already suffering from fever. Nevertheless, neither he nor his wife took it seriously. It was winter. The Bishop was already suffering from cold. It was a one month toil for him; he had been traveling a lot. Therefore, they thought that getting this type of fever was not something to be worried about.

The next day, December 29, was the 32nd Anniversary of his ordination as Bishop. It was customary to hold Holy Communion Service on that day at the Dornakal church, which the Bishop was wont to conduct. He spent the whole night thanking the Lord for leading him 32 years and granting him strength to administer his responsibilities as Bishop at the Diocese, and he prayed for God's grace to sustain him in the future.

As usual, he woke up early in the morning the next day, and finished his meditation and prayer. When he tried to attend the church service, he felt too weak as never before. So, he did not attend the Holy Communion service, and he canceled all other programs for that day. He planned to take rest that day and the following day too. Nevertheless, he was able to do various work from his bed. His weakness turned from bad to worse. But he was enthusiastic. December 31, the last day of the year, was a Sunday. He did not realize that it would be the last day of his life too. He was preparing to conduct the New Year service, and to deliver the New Year sermon. That evening, realizing that he was too weak for this, he decided to take rest at home. Even at that time, he did not realize that he is going to rest in heaven in a few hours. Nor did any of his household realize it.

It was New Year day, 1944. Seventy years had passed by. People in Dornakal were celebrating the New Year. In every house there was New Year's joy!

But in the Bishop's house, there was sudden anxiety and distress. The Bishop's health deteriorated. They urgently summoned Dr. Williams. The doctor felt the Bishop's pulse and checked his heart, and realized that it was weak. Because it was very feeble, he knew that the Bishop's end was drawing near. He called for Dr. Liddell, an Anglo-Indian physician from Singareni, to assist him. Meanwhile, he informed Mrs. Azariah alone about her husband's condition. The Bishop, however, talked enthusiastically as usual, laughed and made others laugh. The clock was ticking. It was past afternoon. Dr. Liddell sent Mrs. Azariah and her daughters Mercy and Grace, and Dr. Williams to have their lunch. Noticing that the Bishop's pulse was getting feebler, and hoping that he would regain strength for one or two hours, he prepared a concoction to boost his nerves. He took a bottle of medicine, and added some drops from it into a glass of water. Being aware of what medicine Dr. Liddell was preparing, the Bishop intently watched him prepare it. He thought something, and began to laugh. "Doctor, when you administer this medicine to me, you are adding a few drops of it in water, but when you take the same medicine, you gulp it," he said, and laughed loudly. The doctor also laughed. Just then, Mrs. Azariah stepped into that room. As he laughed, Azariah reclined on the Lord's loving breast!

His face shone. The clock struck once, indicating that the time was 1:30 p.m. The Diocesan Cathedral bell tolled the death knell to inform the world of the Bishop's departure.

In the Bishop's house, nobody shed tears, nor cried out in grief. Mrs. Azariah and her children patiently bore the great loss of their beloved. There was absolute silence.

But in Dornakal, there were heart-rending cries.

That day and the following day, the Bishop was laid down for final viewing by multitudes of people pouring in. Men and women stood in queue to behold the Bishop's lit-up face that was brimming with grace. They kept coming and going.

At 5:00 p.m. on the second of the month, 1944, they laid him to rest in a vault behind the Dornakal Cathedral that was a magnificent symbol of the Bishop's lifelong ministry. "The pilgrim was placed in his vault. Its window faced the rising sun. The room was named PEACE. He would sleep there until the day dawns. When it dawns, he would rise up to sing praise hymns."[7]

"His eyes shall see his Redeemer."

A REVIEW

Samuel

SAMUEL was a prophet. He was a seer, a priest, and an administrator. He was a man of honesty and integrity. He did not fall or slip from his upright life. He was also a judge. He was a servant of God. He had received the grace of God. By the command of God, he anointed kings. He loosened the Philistines' grip over Israel, and toiled to unite the tribes of Israel to form one kingdom.

How appropriate was the name Samuel that his mother had chosen for the Bishop! In India and globally, in the life of the Church, who deserved these praises and the attainment of high offices in his job than the one who bore the holy name of Samuel?

Azariah

There was a man called Azariah. The Spirit of God descended on him. He warned King Asa and the tribe of Judah. People turned to God in repentance. The land was cleansed. (II Chronicles 15).

There were two captains called Azariah. Each of them was a captain over a hundred soldiers. They, along with some others, toured all over the country and marshalled the Levites and the elders of the tribes, and gathered them all at Jerusalem. All who had gathered made a covenant with the king. Queen Athaliah, who personified evil, was killed. The rightful prince Joash became the king. (II Chronicles 23).

There was a high priest called Azariah. Being zealous for

the Temple and the ordinances of God, he resisted King Uzziah who came to offer incense in God's Temple. (II Chronicles 26).

There were two others named Azariah in the scriptures. Both of them belonged to the priestly tribe of Levi. They, along with others who were chosen to cleanse the temple, entered the temple, and cleansed the temple by removing all the filth in it. And the Levites carried the filth to the brook Kidron. (II Chronicles 29).

There was yet another Azariah who was also a high priest. He rejoiced to see the excess of tithes and offerings that people brought into the temple when the priests and the Levites kept the ordinances of the Lord at the command of King Hezekiah. (II Chronicles 31).

Ezra, a priest and a scribe, read the Book of the Law before the people. One of the priests named Azariah, along with some others, the Levites, read from the Law of God, and gave the sense, so that the people understood the reading. When the people heard the exposition, they were convicted of their sins, repented and mourned, and wept. (Nehemiah 8).

Perhaps Rev. Vedhanayagam, a priest of the Tirunelveli Church, knew beforehand that his son Azariah too would be filled by the Spirit of God to warn the church authorities and administrators, and cleanse the Church. Did he envisage that one day his son would be a minister of the YMCA, and establish, in a small scale, but with a large vision, the Indian Missionary Society, the National Missionary Society and other Societies? Or, would he have envisaged that his son would go as a missionary, and become a Bishop of a Diocese that started small, but grew by leaps and bounds, and that Azariah would travel all over Andhra and India preaching the gospel, bringing hundreds of thousands of people to the heavenly 'Jerusalem', unto Jesus? Would he have envisaged that his son would become a pastor and a chief pastor, a zealous Churchman teaching and preserving the Church's ordinances? Could he have believed that his little son would become a valiant warrior fighting to get rid of the evil of divisions in the Church, the body of Christ, by removing its various underlying evils like fervor for principles and traditions, obstinacy, church-pride, and selfishness? Did Vedhanayagam foreknow that his son, like King Hezekiah and the High Priest Azariah, would hold lifelong spiritual meetings and days of silent meditation for servants of God, motivating and encouraging them and helping them to work hard as faithful shepherds? And, as King Hezekiah and the High Priest Azariah knew, by experience, the truth that they need not demand tithes and offerings; so also, pastors and catechists who delight in the law of the Lord, and walk in the way of God's laws, need not demand offerings from their flocks, saying, "Give Offering!". Did Rev. Vedhanayagam of Vellalanvilai village ever foresee that his son would consider the Bible as his food and as the basis of his life; and, that true to his name Vedhanayagam (Bible hero), he would make the teaching of the scriptures as his primary job; and that he would help in Bible translation, Bible distribution, and such work; and that he would author Bible commentaries, expositions, and explanations? Was Vedhanayagam aware that his son would call people to repentance through his scriptural teaching as did the priest Azariah and the other priests with Ezra the Scribe?

Vedhanayagam did not know these things earlier; nor did he become aware of these later. Nevertheless, he named his son as 'Azariah' along with the name 'Samuel'. How did he choose this name? It seems nobody by the name of Azariah was in the CMS churches or SPG churches when Azariah was born. There was no missionary by that name. There was nobody by the name Azariah in Meignanapuram and Pannaivilai, nor in his wife's native villages. Then, why this name?

"...and you shall call his name John. And you will have joy and gladness...he will be great before the Lord...and he will be filled with the Holy Spirit..." Luke 1: 13-17.

"...None of your relatives is called by this name"..."and wrote, 'His name is John.'"

Let us assume that Rev. Vedhanayagam, unaware, and prompted by the Holy Spirit of God, in the same manner as above, named his son 'Azariah'. His three names Vedhanayagam Samuel Azariah seemed to proclaim in advance his manifold services.

Bishop

Among the Indian Church leaders, none arose as 'the mighty man of valor' Azariah. Very few worked as hard and efficiently in every department of the Church life as Azariah did.

From his school days and through his old age as Bishop until he reached the presence of his heavenly Father, one character that stood out was his genuine devotion to Christ. Other characters that supported this character were: As he often said, meditating God's Word; Supplication and prayer; and Divine Holy Communion. The fruits of his life were: Passion for Evangelism; Thirst for souls; Strong liking for the well-being of the Church; Strong desire for Church unity; Holiness in his personal life; Love for fellow human beings; Deep love for His Savior.

How can such a Bishop not be accepted by people as their 'father in God'? He was a loving father, a caring and protective father, and a chastening father. Those who did not accept his chastening could not accept him as father. Such people criticized him, saying, "He was a dictator". In committee meetings, when some people wanted to have their own way, Azariah objected to it; and they accused him, saying, "He wants to have his own way". Generally, an evil that prevailed in church committees all over was that some people attended committee meetings with their own agenda on problems and issues. Some attend committees with their own agenda. There were just four or five persons who took part in committee deliberations. Others mechanically raised their hands. They kept silent in committee meetings as if they were dumb. Those who came to committee meetings with hidden agenda might have already influenced these silent members even before the meetings by talking to them; or they might have cajoled them or threatened them into submission, or used other means to make them raise their hands to vote for them. When problems reached a critical stage and went for voting, these silent members would raise their hands or mutter 'yes' or 'no' as their influencers wanted. It is not a hard task for the silent members to nod their heads. Such antics did not work with Azariah.

The moment he recognizes those who act according to their own plans, Azariah would scold them. He would trouble those 'vote-catchers'. He would deal harshly with those who canvass. "Those who plan their own agenda before they attend committee meetings commit the unpardonable sin of blaspheming the Holy Spirit if they had taken part in the Holy Communion ahead of the Committee Meeting and in the opening prayer seeking the guidance and counsel of the Holy Spirit," said Azariah often.

His short-temper was his shortcoming. It's a pity that all bishops may be subject to this shortcoming. Among some 15 bishops I knew, only two were exceptions to this criticism. In the history of the Church, among thousands of bishops, just a few were described as free from anger. We do not know if the heavy burden they have to bear as bishops make them to be so. Our earlier description of Azariah was: "He spoke tenderly. He was not an angry man." Later, as mentioned above, if he saw evil entering committee meetings, he appeared to lose his patience. Nevertheless, his good qualities of forgiveness, mercy and love, would drive away his anger in a moment.

He did not like people approaching him with fear and trembling. So, whoever met him, he would first drive away their fear by opening his conversation in a humorous way. Yet, it seems even missionaries approached him with a little fear. When we read his numerous letters we perceive that he was a meek and humble-hearted man. Therefore, it is a mystery why people feared to approach such a meek and humble man. One thing is certain: he desired that servants of God must work for the development of Dornakal, for people's welfare, and for the glory of God, as he did. He had determined that there was no place for dishonest workers in Dornakal.

He loved Dornakal to that extent. When he was the Secretary of the Indian Missionary Society, he had the opportunity to get a high position in the International YMCA. This was the time that he had felt he should go to Dornakal and work there as an ordinary missionary. The YMCA job would have brought him abundant fame, praise, and income. Dornakal offered him low salary, life without comforts, hard work, and the risk of being unknown. Azariah chose Dornakal and its attendant sufferings.

Probably, he loved Tirunelveli more than he loved Dornakal. He showed great concern for the welfare of his 'mother church'. After Bishop William's sudden death in June 1914, Azariah supervised Tirunelveli Diocese until December 1915, when Bishop Waller assumed the position of Tirunelveli Bishop. He considered this as blessing for him to take care of both 'the mother' and 'the daughter' simultaneously. Later, when Bishop Tubbs was transferred to Rangoon (Yangon), Tirunelveli beckoned Azariah. Eminent persons in Tirunelveli like J. Anbudaiyan, Daniel Thomas, D. Rajendram, J. T. Sreenivasagam, P. A. Thangasamy, A. C. Paul, M. Asirvatham, R. V. Asirvatham and G. T. Selwyn greatly desired to make Azariah as the Bishop in Tirunelveli. Although Azariah liked the idea, he chose not to get the pride of position as 'Tirunelveli Bishop'. He chose his Dornakal which was full of poor, simple people, and which was at the lowest rung of civilization, worldly glory, and education.[1]

If we keep on writing, this book will become thicker! We thank and praise God for the blessing of the treasure of Azariah that He gave to Tirunelveli, Dornakal, the Indian Church, and the global church. Praying to God that He Who gave 'Azariah' then, may now raise many 'Azariahs' across the globe; let us surrender ourselves and all our possessions to God.

1. Letters of J. Anbudaiyan, 1928.

APPENDIX

Azariah's father Rev. Vedhanayagam

Most people consider that it was his mother who laid the foundation for Bishop Azariah's future development. Because his father Rev. Vedhanayagam died when Azariah was a little boy, nobody knows the contribution his father made for the development of Azariah's excellent qualities. Therefore, we give a summary of what Azariah himself stated about his father:

> *"My father died on June 23, 1889. Any son would take pride in having a father like mine. He firmly believed that our conduct should be in righteousness and justice as far as we relate to the oppressed and the helpless people, and others like them. His conduct revealed not even a little selflessness. He was great in spending and being spent for his Master and His Church. My heart is filled with rightful pride and gratitude for the privilege of being his son. May our loving heavenly Father fill me with His Spirit that I may also serve God, as my father did, in all humility. My father loved me a lot. When I was a little boy, I used to sit with him to have my meals. Yet, I was very scared of him. My father's one stern look was equal to six canings from my mother! The privileges I enjoyed in my house were in no way better than what a village boy would enjoy in his house. I received the same kind of punishment that a village boy would receive, or even more! That was my father!"* [1]

The Rev. John Thomas of Meignanapuram, in a Report

1. In a letter dated June 22, 1898 in English – translated by the author.

dated February 12, 1869, a few days after Vedhanayagam's Ordination to the Diaconate, writes as follows:

"Vedhanayagam Thomas' long experience admirably qualifies him for his present responsible position, where he has charge of 750 souls. The first service in the morning was entirely conducted by him. It was well-attended. Nothing could have been more appropriate than the admirable sermon which he preached from the second chapter of Jeremiah, verses five and six. It was a very carefully prepared sermon, but delivered extempore. In any part of England, had I casually gone to a country parish church, I should have rejoiced to hear so clear and earnest a discourse. I could not help feeling the deepest gratitude to God for raising up in the Native Church in Tinnevelly so able a Minister of the New Testament, not of the letter only, but of the Spirit." [2]

2. Church Missionary Record, 1870 – Annual Report for 1869 and diary.

They are as follows-Tamil

1. History of Nazareth Mission – 1950
2. Christian Gospel to a Hindu friend – 1952
3. Prophert Isaiah - Drama – 1945
4. Life history of Billy Graham – 1956
5. History of Christiannagaram Mission – 1960
6. World Christian Union – 1962
7. Prophets of Old Testaments – Eliah and Eliza – 1965
8. Marayaviruntha Manikka karkal – Part – 1 – 1970
9. Oyyangudi Church History – 1971
10. Vellarikaoorani Church history – 1972
11. Life history of Bishop Azariah – 1974
12. Life history of North Nellai Apostle Rev.Ragland – Part – 1- 1974
13. Life history of Nellai Appostel Rev.Rhenius – 1975
14. Indian Church history – Part – 1 – 1975
15. Life history of David Sundaranantham – 1976
16. Marayaviruntha Manikka karkal – Part – 2 – 1976
17. Thiruchabaiyin parisuththa vattigal Panniruvar – 1976
18. Indian Church history – Part – 2 – 1977
19. Life history of Rev.John Devasagayam – 1977
20. Life history of South Nellai Appostel Rev.John Thomas – 1977
21. Life history of Rev.Margoschis – 1977
22. Life history of North Nellai Apostle Rev.Ragland – Part – 2 – 1977
23. Life history of Bishop Sargent –
24. Indian Church history – Part – 3 – 1978
25. Life history of Bishop Robert Caldwell – 1980
26. Life history of Cloridal – 1977
27. Life history of Nambiammal – 1977

28. Life history of John William – 1983
29. Ratha satchigalagiya thairiya senai – 1978
30. Antha arputham nadantha kathai – 1979
31. Raththa Muththirai – 1981
32. King's heart in Lord's hand – 1978
33. History of Appostels – 1978 etc

9 798889 590026

Printed by Libri Plureos GmbH in Hamburg,
Germany